H.R. people talk about policies and procedures. O.D. people talk about "to-be" states and building teams. I.T. people talk about leveraging technology. Eric's blend of experience in all of these areas makes him uniquely qualified to talk about H.R. Integration. <u>The H.R. Predicament</u> truly gives a roadmap to bring them all together!

> Scott Mannis, PhD
> Sr. Vice President Human Resources
> Kellwood Corporation

<u>The H.R. Predicament</u> is a practical, no-nonsense guide for enhancing the effectiveness and impact of H.R. It's an interesting, jargon-free read that's a must for any H.R. practitioner dedicated to reinventing and refocusing the function.

> Lois M. Huggins
> Chief Human Resources Officer,
> Senior Vice President
> Rehabilitation Institute of Chicago

The H.R. Predicament!

Balancing Functional Excellence and Process Integration…

…Practical H.R. Strategies.

Written by
Eric Schneider

Produced & Distributed by
I Am Enterprises, LLC

Contents

Acknowledgements

A Sincere thanks to my family, friends and colleagues for their support and encouragement.

Thanks to the Aberdeen Group, Marshall Goldsmith and SHRM for granting permission to reference/reprint their research.

Thanks to Kelly Eisenhart (my wife) for the editorial and publishing support needed to make this book happen.

A final thanks to Anne Offner, Lois Huggins, Steve Malec and Scott Mannis for their quotations and contributions.

With gratitude to the great bosses I've had who taught me so much and to the not-so-great ones, for I learned much from them as well.

Disclaimers

The ideas and opinions shared in this book are the views of the author, based on a wide array of experiences, interviews and impressions accumulated through exposure to many sources and are not specifically attributable to any previous employer, client, student or colleague unless noted as such in the writing or credits.

This book focuses on process optimization through simplifying, standardizing and integrating Human Resources functions. It does not address specific H.R. compliance to state or federal laws around employment, regulatory compliance (which can vary greatly by state, country and industry) or other litigation risks relating to Human Resources. As with any business changes, review all applicable process/procedure modifications with your organizations' legal counsel prior to implementation.

Book Introduction

There it is again. It usually starts out low. Perhaps it begins as a faint growl from the nearby office buildings, or the factory down the street. It slowly grows until it has reached a steady roar. Not just any roar, the kind with teeth! I'm talking about the biting criticism that seems to surround the H.R. department at so many companies.

The H.R. leadership team just can't seem to figure it out. The Compensation department benchmarks toe-to-toe with elite companies. The O.D. department is brimming with bright minds and progressive ideas. The H.R. Generalists work as hard as anyone in the entire company and are passionate about supporting their internal clients. And nobody handles the volume of work day-in and day-out like the Recruiting department. So what's wrong? How can H.R. be so good in most (or in some companies even all) of its functions and still be met with such skepticism by the rest of the organization?

There is one word that defines both the problem and the solution for most Human Resources departments. It's something that Procurement, Manufacturing/Operations and Warehousing came to understand when the Supply Chain Management craze swept through the United States during the 1990's. Even Sales and Marketing caught on as *CRM* became fashionable.

I'm talking about process INTEGRATION! It seems so obvious, yet time and again H.R. departments strive and even obtain functional excellence but fail to address process integration. And that is what drives their internal clients crazy. In some cases, H.R. leaders are so blinded by the shine of their functional excellence that they fail to recognize that what the company is crying for is simple integration across all aspects of Human Resources.

Now, don't get me wrong, I'm not suggesting such a feat is easy. Great H.R. leaders, and sometimes even CEO's who are dialed in to managing their human assets, have struggled to make it happen. There are some HRIS and ERP software companies that have tried to create a platform for helping companies integrate processes across H.R. functions. Certainly this technology can help. However, if an H.R. department doesn't simplify its processes, have strong data management practices, and foster a staff culture/mentality for working across functions, then no amount of technology is going to bring about INTEGRATION.

The purpose of this book is to share some thoughts, ideas and insights into transforming your Human Resources department into a well integrated operation. If you are one of the few who are part of an H.R. organization that has already achieved such excellence, then hopefully the information in this book will serve as a point of validation. As for the rest (and majority) of us who are somewhere on the integration continuum, we hope to provide practical suggestions that are based more on thoughtful ideas rather than blue pie-in-the-sky solutions that require unrealistic cost and resources.

We'll explore three primary steps to building a foundation for an integrated H.R. function. These include:

- Applying an H.R. Data Management philosophy, regardless of available technology,

- Deploying one single Proficiency Catalog that governs all Recruiting, Compensation, O.D. and Generalist processes, and

- Techniques for including (and leveraging) those secondary processes that often create a drag on H.R. operations.

Applying these concepts in a practical manner will transform those current angry growls into roars of applause!

Section I:

H.R. Information

*Building the Foundation
for Process Integration*

Section Introduction

Are you one of the very few who have all your H.R. data in one system along with one unique definition that is shared and agreed upon for each data point across your entire organization? If so, you can skip this section. BUT, just to be safe, first ask yourself these questions before electing to move on:

- Do Payroll, Compensation, Legal, HRIS and all of your Benefits Providers have a clearly defined (and adhered to) definition of what constitutes an employees' *last day worked*?

- Does your company have a well defined and up to date data dictionary for the fields that make up employee records and H.R. related information?

- Are all Reporting Relationships and Organization Hierarchies stored in one place? Are they easily synchronized across all other systems and processes without manual or multiple entries?

- Are standard naming conventions used for Job titles and departments in a consistent manner with minimal overlap?

- Has a formal catalog of job titles been established that is manageable and fully rationalized?

- Have any of your H.R. or payroll functions received any SOX violations or been cited by the audit department?

Unless you are in the clear on all of the above items, it might be worth your time to read on...

Note: The concepts addressed in Section I are of a more technical nature around H.R. Technology and Data Management. While readers who do not have a technology background might find Section I more difficult to follow, this foundational information is essential to capturing maximum benefit from the H.R. Process Optimization discussed in Section II and Section III.

Chapter 1: Managing Data Definitions

It doesn't matter whether you have automated processes and state of the art technology; if you are not managing organizational and employee information correctly, process integration will always elude you.

How many data points does your organization maintain for each employee record? Probably more than you think! The consensus among numerous I.T. and H.R. professionals and consultants I've spoken with is that companies generally maintain (albeit informally) approximately 400-500 data points for each employee. An initial response might be that your organization maintains nowhere near this amount. However, when you factor in things such as "effective" dates for things such as promotions, pay changes, titles, etc., the quantity of data points grows quickly. Unless your HRIS technology is advanced and systems platform highly integrated, the thought of managing data continuity across the entire organization can be overwhelming.

There is an alternative, especially if your company still maintains employee data on multiple systems, or has varied processes across operating units. The truth is, only a subset of the 400-500 data points really need to be standardized to ensure sound H.R. analytics and process continuity. The solution is to develop a *mini master* record for employee data. Colleagues I've spoken to generally conclude that companies can get by with a *mini master* comprised of about 50-80 data points.

So what does this really mean? It is simply the list of data points that you will use to gain company- wide clarity and alignment on:

- A commonly held definition
- Parameters and specifications use
- Understood checks and controls to ensure data is accurate.

 **Information is what drives HR processes. So, the more your data is defined and aligned, the better your Human Resources Department will be.**

H.R. Data Inventory

Begin by taking an initial inventory of all employee data points. Include information from Finance/Accounting, benefits providers, employee directories, Property Management (Real Estate Dept.), as well as the conventional HRIS data. The data dictionary is the tool you'll use to manage the final *mini master*. However, it can also be used to build the initial inventory of employee data. For the initial information gathering, only the name and ideally the systems where the data point is stored/used is needed.

Once the H.R. organization has agreed which 50-80 data points should comprise the *mini master*, proceed with filling in the rest of the information for each entry in the data dictionary. We'll examine this in more detail later in this chapter.

Identifying the *Mini-Master*

In an ideal world, there would not be a need for a mini-master. Continuity and controls would be in place for all 400 – 500 employee data points. But we know that this is not practical; that is unless your organization has a large staff of resources dedicated solely to managing H.R. information. Therefore, your governing factor in determining which data elements comprise the *mini master* should be based first and foremost on what is realistically a manageable list! Balance this with assessing what information is common to all processes and systems. At first glance, your list of data points won't appear very sexy or of great impact. But remember, these are important because they serve as the foundational building blocks for establishing process and information continuity across all H.R. functions and systems. If these basic data points aren't fully controlled, then process integration is compromised. As you build consensus throughout the stakeholders and H.R. functional silos, resist the temptation to appease the calls for over complicating the mini-master. Illustration 1.0 shows a few of the most basic data points that will serve as the building blocks for establishing a *mini master* record.

ILLUSTRATION 1.0

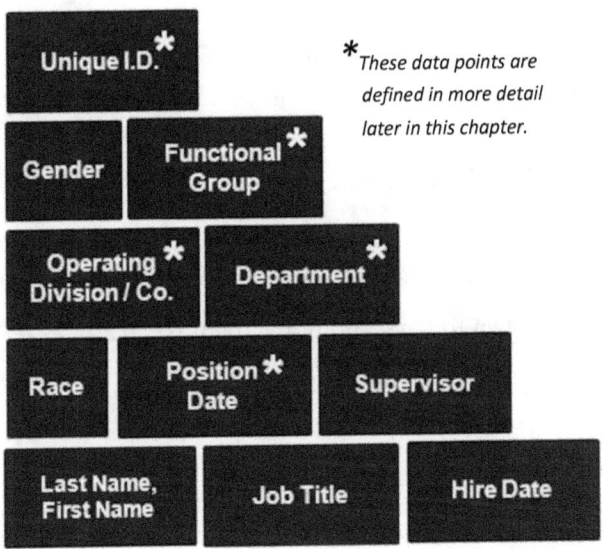

Creating a Data Dictionary

Once the data points that will make up the *mini master* are defined, the next step is to collect all the details needed to ensure clarity, and then apply the controls necessary to maintain integrity. The data dictionary serves as the single document for accomplishing this. The data dictionary can be used to clarify and track the following attributes around each data point included in the *mini master*:

- The official (field) name
- An inventory of any alternate or "also known as" names
- A standard definition
- Systems/Applications in which the data point is used
- A business owner.

Illustration 1.2 is an example of a data dictionary. You may elect to have additional fields (such as comments/notes or perhaps a change tracking date).

ILLUSTRATION 1.2

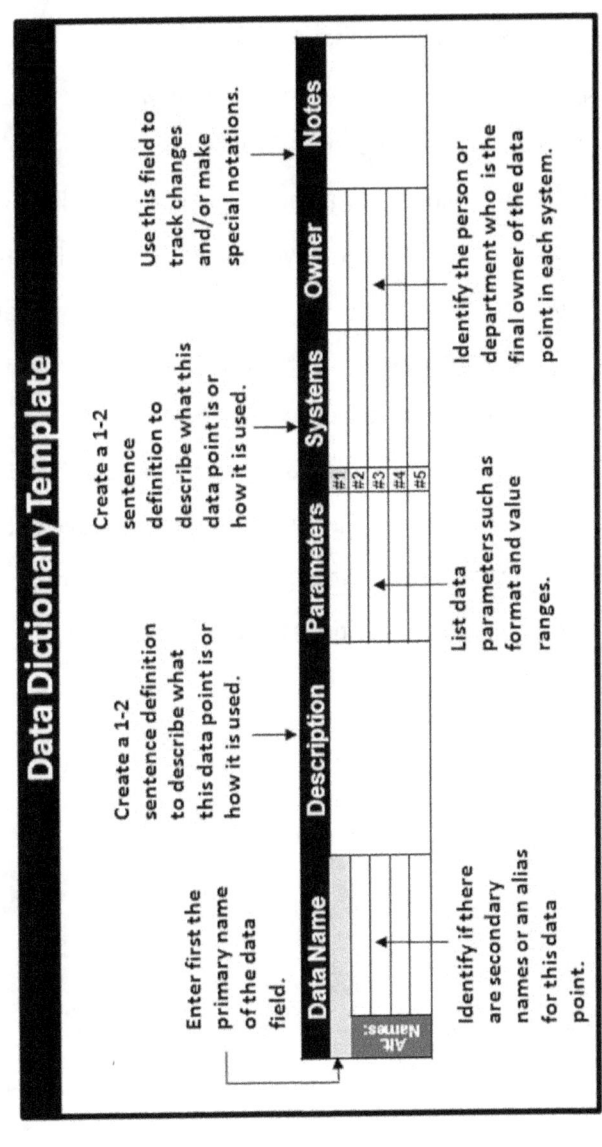

It's important that each data point has both an official *System of Record* (S.O.R.) and a business owner. If not all systems are interfaced, then one must be designated the dominant repository over all others. Ideally, this will be the system in which the employee record is maintained. If for some reason a particular data point is not part of the employee master record, then the *System of Record* should be the one in which changes are first entered/processed. Once the SOR is assigned, it becomes much easier to realign H.R. processes to ensure updates happen consistently and efficiently. Establishing a *System of Record* also allows for easier pro-active data audits, as well as troubleshooting and issue resolution when data integrity questions arise.

Chapter 2: Organizing H.R. Information

Once the list is compiled, it's helpful to categorize the data into three or four types. This is useful when establishing/assigning an owner (and stakeholders) to each data element as mentioned in the previous chapter. The I.T. world refers to this as developing a *schema*, which is a method for organizing groups of data points into an organized structure. *Schemas* add logic to how the information is stored and retrieved. I recommend using the following groupings:

- ***Core Data***: name, unique identifier, job, age, race gender, etc.

- **Pay/Benefit Data**: salary, Coverage plans and enrollments, bonus/incentive programs, pay related accounting codes, etc.

- **Talent Data**: education, external work history, performance ratings, skills and attributes (qualifications), development plans.

- **Organizational Information**: department, organizational workgroups (more on that later), business divisions, locations, etc.

Core Data

Core Data is the basic employee information used in nearly all H.R. processes and even business transactions that involve employee information. It's the most basic and straightforward data. However, it also holds the highest risk for discrepancies and redundancy. Because this information is maintained across so many systems and processes (and often manually entered/re-entered), the probability of inaccuracies goes up considerably. That's why it is so important to have both an official *System of Record* and an assigned Business Owner for this information. Below is a sampling of the basic employee information that is common to most processes and systems that utilize employee information:

TABLE 1.1

Core Data	
Last Name, First Name	Gender
Current Job Title	Race
Grading Level / Banding	Age
Department	Hire Date
Contact Information	Supervisor
Unique Identifier	Operating Unit/Division

When identifying what to classify as "*core*" data, think back to the old days of personnel files. Much of the *core data* is likely to include most (or possibly even all) of the *mini master* Information, plus history when applicable. Also include the start/end date information around things like job and department changes, and other personnel transactions. Other items in addition to the *mini master* data fields to be given consideration for classification as *core data* might include:

- Job History Start/End Dates
- Job Title History
- Transaction (reason) codes
- Additional location information.

Finally, don't leave out third party or outsourced systems and services.

Pay/Benefit Data

As more payroll and benefits processes are being outsourced, companies are finding their employee pay/benefit residing outside of the internal HRIS systems. While the service providers may offer greater efficiency, don't be lulled into thinking that this data doesn't need to be managed internally. The outsourced payroll and benefits processes rely heavily on much of the information that is in your *mini master* in order to accurately conduct transactions. Furthermore, some of the most powerful H.R. analytics that can drive real value to the overall organization involve combining the Pay/Benefit information with other data points maintained within H.R. (i.e. pay vs. performance trends, total cost of labor analysis, etc.)

So, while the information may be housed in the benefit provider's system, it is essential that you: 1) establish the same documentation and controls around this information that is done for the other H.R. data, and 2) apply the same principles of integration and automation addressed later in this book for other H.R. functional areas.

Organizational Information

Ask department heads what their greatest challenge is when it comes to managing organizational information and many will say it's trying to keep organizational charts up to date. As Steve Malec, currently a Director of Employee Relations at Ryerson, can attest, *"Maintaining Organizational Charts at most companies is an afterthought, or at the very least an additional activity that occurs independent of the employee transaction itself"*. Having your H.R.

organizational data formatted properly is one way of making this easier and more accurate.

Departments often want their organizational data uniquely subdivided into finely splintered names and groupings, making it more difficult to provide meaningful information. This also has an adverse impact on talent management efforts as the splintering of department names can make the grouping of like roles/skill groups more complicated.

Although putting the company on notice that H.R. processes and analytics will only span three organizational tiers (not reporting relationships) may not be a popular message initially, it won't be long before they are thanking you. Within a few months (as data cycles through the improved processes) things like employee directories, organizational charts, talent/performance management procedures and standard H.R. analytics/reporting will be notably improved.

Again, we are not talking about reporting relationships such as supervisor or manager, but rather the departmental tiers that make up the framework of the company's organization. A common template for a three tier hierarchy might look something like this:

Tier #1: Business Segments/Divisions: These refer to the types or lines of business a company engages in. For example, a dairy company might have division names such as Milk, Butter, Yogurt and Cheese.   Or, an apparel business could be comprised of Segments like Footwear, Accessories and Clothing.

Tier #2: Functional Groups: These are the operational areas that comprise each Division/Segment (Tier #1). For most companies they are things like Marketing, Manufacturing, Sales, Procurement, Customer Service, Accounting/Finance, etc.

Tier #3: Departmental Unit: The last tier is comprised of the individual departments that make up the functional groups in Tier 2.   In this example, the Manufacturing functional group could have Organizational Units like Production, Warehouse, Distribution, Maintenance, Safety, etc.

Barring major organizational realignments such as divestitures and acquisitions, these three tiers typically stay relatively static for most companies. This means that data maintenance is likely less frequent. It's the details below Tier #3 that departments often want to change practically every time a position is vacated and filled. If departments like Manufacturing, Sales, Marketing, Procurement, Finance or any other group wants further gradient, then it must be upon them to track that level of detail on their own. But again, they will soon find that by simply combining the above three tiers with reporting relationship data will give them all the information they need. AND, once H.R.'s internal clients see how much easier employee transactional forms become, they'll be thanking you! In Section II we'll discuss how this and other simple measures go a long way towards streamlining H.R. processes and replacing customer growls into howls of appreciation!

Another data point to include as part of your company's organizational information is the *Physical Work Location*. For some companies, a certain amount of care must be given to how detailed this data point should be. For an organization with many hundred employees who work from a home office, using a physical work address might result in too much gradient; making reports less meaningful, and the task of keeping information up to date too arduous. In such cases the location field may need to be rolled up to a city, state or other geographic metric.

With this approach, organizational charts and reports can be constructed in a concise and consistent manner by using the *Schema* shown in Illustration 1.2:

ILLUSTRATION 1.2

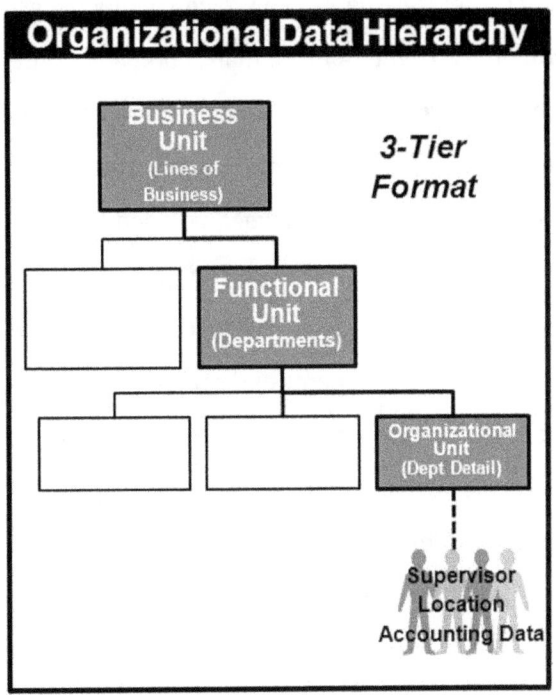

This is the beginning of the foundation for integration across H.R. functional silos.   All H.R. process data will start to speak the same language.

Beware of Accounting Structures

Accounting data and H.R. hierarchies can be a bit like oil and vinegar. There are times when mixed together carefully that accounting data can be quite useful in efforts to display organizational and business structures. But make no mistake; that they are not the same. Things like cost centers/elements can provide additional gradient to workforce analytics, but for many companies, internal accounts and organizational hierarchies are not a one-to-one relationship across the entire organization. For example, there may be employees assigned to one department organizationally, but charged to a different internal account. This tends to happen for long term projects, special assignments and sometimes as a cost allocation for certain support functions. Likewise, similar situations may occur if your organization includes temporary and/or contract employees as part of headcount and organizational reporting.

To Summarize, good organizational data is the foundation for ALL workforce analytics. In the end, the credibility of your headcount, diversity, labor cost, turnover and even recruiting reports will all be impacted either favorably or unfavorably by the accuracy of your organizational data. Keep your organizational structures practical and you'll be on your way to better reporting and happier internal clients!

Talent Data

Talent data is the information that, when combined with *core data*, is typically used to make assessments in such processes as bench strength analysis & succession planning, performance management and talent management initiatives. Some organizations also include portions of pay/benefits data as part of the talent management processes as well. Information typically categorized as talent data may include:

TABLE 1.2

Talent Data	
Education / Certifications	Development Plans
Previous/External Employment	Ability to Relocate
Proficiencies: Strengths	Language Skills
Proficiencies: Development Needs	Performance Ratings
Accomplishments	Readiness For Promotion
Career Interests	Succession Decisions
Geographic Availability	Travel Availability

The main question to ask when identifying your organization's talent data set is: What information about the employee do I need to very practically, yet effectively, conduct an accurate talent inventory and then develop succession plans? Not enough information obviously translates into a weak talent management program. However, there is also a real risk in building talent processes that are too cumbersome to effectively execute. We'll discuss this in more detail in Chapters 5 & 6.

For those companies without a talent management application that is integrated with other H.R. systems, gathering talent related data for your succession planning and *Talent Development* processes can be an arduous task. When there is too much administrative burden placed on the employee or his/her manager, the organization will approach talent management initiatives half heartedly. The trick is to find a way to assemble and pre-populate as much of this information as possible without unduly tying up limited H.R. resources (lest your internal clients will complain that H.R. is fooling around with talent management activities rather than taking care of their daily business needs!).

The solution then, at least in part, is to "mine" the data from sources where it might already exist, rather than having to engage the employee, line manager and H.R. resources to manually assemble it. While there may not be one single place to source the talent data, some clusters of information are likely being collected -

sometimes even electronically - in other functions beyond O.D. processes.

For example, most recruiting departments rely on some form of online application processing, applicant tracking or resume repository. At the very least, the applicant data is keyed into a tracking spreadsheet. Talent information available electronically through applicant tracking tools might include education levels, certifications and licenses, and external or previous employment history. Some applications may even store data on language skills, international experience and employee's geographic/mobility preferences.

Tuition Reimbursement processes can also be a source for bulk collection of talent data. Often, the processing of tuition reimbursement is tucked away in the Finance/Accounting department and the data may not be top of mind to the H.R. staff. But, with a little digging, you should be able to glean some information that will help fill in blanks in your talent data set.

Last, if your company does not have a centralized Learning Management System (LMS), do some digging to determine what is being used around the organization. Chances are Sales, Operations, Compliance/Regulatory and possibly Marketing departments are tracking employee courses/seminars/workshops in either the training deliver system or at least a spreadsheet. Chapter 9 provides more information on the role training systems can play in overall H.R. process integration.

As we'll discuss in Section II, there is a trend in businesses today to make talent management processes far more complex than what is really needed. The more practical and low maintenance your talent management processes are, the greater likelihood the organization will embrace them to the point of success! Having good H.R. data management practices and integrated H.R. processes is THE KEY to making this happen!

Summary

Illustration 1.3 summarizes the basic structure for organizing H.R. information into four basic groups, with the *mini master* comprised of individual data points from each.

ILLUSTRATION 1.3

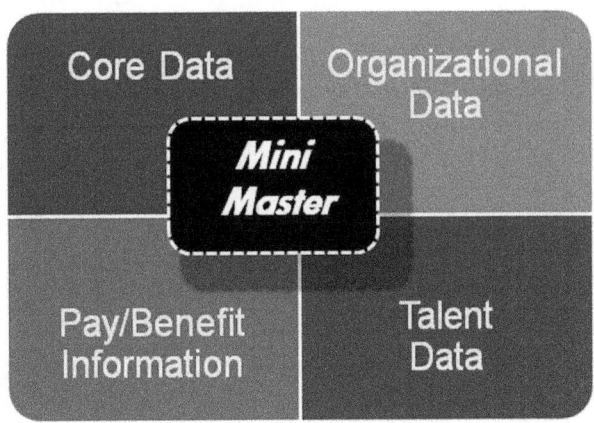

Remember, even if your *Pay/Benefit* functions are outsourced or handled by a third party platform, it is still important to make sure the data points are properly mapped/documented and governed by the *mini master*.

 Make sure processes and data capabilities are at the same level. Don't let processes become more sophisticated than what your data can deliver.

Chapter 3: H.R. Data Governance

While more and more is written on *Data Management* for Supply Chain, Sales and Finance data, employee data seldom gets more than a brief mention. Yet there are enough critical *"Do's, Don'ts* and *How To's"* on the subject to fill yet another book. Here are some measures you can take to establish basic data governance for employee and organizational information.

The Hidden Benefit of Regulatory Compliance

We all know that the Sarbanes-Oxley Act of 2002 has been a tremendous windfall for accounting, audit and consulting firms. For sure it's created a bureaucratic drag on departments and functions throughout most companies. But, the pain of SOX compliance can also be an effective tool in the effort to standardize H.R. data and processes. In simplest terms SOX compliance for H.R. is centered on:

1. Identifying process and information owners

2. Limiting access to who can add-change-delete employee information, and

3. Establishing controls around overall data accuracy.

Having these measures and policies in place makes it easier to deploy the changes outlined throughout this book that are necessary to achieve process integration. Let's examine some of them a bit further.

Data Owners

Every data point for employee and organizational information should have a person/position, or at the very least a department, who is the assigned owner. The data owner is responsible for:

- Helping determine a standard definition for the data point

- Becoming the authority on how this information is used across multiple processes and the nuances of how they inter-relate or intersect

- How this information CAN and CANNOT be used

- And, in some cases, WHO is allowed to view and use this data point.

Being the owner doesn't necessarily mean that they have sole control over how the data point gets defined and used. In most cases there will be multiple Stakeholders who also have a deep reliance (and say so) on the same piece of information. However, the owner is the person that serves as the final voice once all considerations have been examined, or for those times when a single "Go-To" person is needed on decisions. As noted in Chapter 1, remember to document the owner in the data dictionary. Documenting the stakeholders may also be an effective means of easing concerns some might have about not being the actual data owner. Seeing their name/department at least associated with the data point is enough reassurance that they still have a say in controlling the information.

Forms Management

If data is what drives H.R. processes, then forms are the highway that helps them reach the destination. There is nothing that you can do to impact overall data continuity more than to establish continuity across all H.R. forms. If you have online or self service technology, then this task becomes much easier. If you rely on manual forms and electronic documents, then follow these simple guidelines to help ensure the consistency of information on H.R. forms:

- Take every opportunity to make all input field a drop down menu or some form of finite/fixed – list. This can be achieved easily with the features available in most spreadsheet applications and eForms software.

- Ensure that the same selections are used for a given field or data point across all H.R. processes (More on this in Chapter 6.).

- When possible use "if-then" formulas in spreadsheet based forms to pre-populate fields with default information based on data entered in another part of the form. Again, such functionality is standard in most spreadsheet applications.

Taking Pro-Active Measures

Typically a SOX plan includes routine audits of H.R. data as a means of demonstrating that controls and monitoring are in place. These activities are in addition to the annual SOX review/audit. There are a few hotspots in particular where the accuracy of H.R. data always seems to be a challenge. These include maintaining accurate reporting relationships and job titles, along with the challenge of missing information deemed "non-mandatory" (i.e. education, language skills, work location, etc.) on some forms.

 If information is what drives HR processes, then forms are the highways that help them reach their destination.

Recovering Missing Data

A monthly audit of new hire records in your H.R. system can reduce missing information. Begin by printing out a report that lists new employees hired (or for which a new record has been established) in the past month. Highlight any records that are missing non-mandatory information. (Again, for most companies, these are data points used for talent related processes, but are not required fields for processing new employees. So, in many cases this is going to be information categorized as talent data during the exercises earlier in this chapter. Finally, invest the time to reference these employees' applications and/or resumes housed in the Recruiting department's applicant system (or physical files), to find the missing information. The hiring manager information may also be available in the recruiting documentation, which can plug holes in reporting relationship data. Yes, this is a bit of manual work up front. But, as you'll see later in this book, the small time increments spent up front to fill in the blanks will eventually save countless hours throughout the overall H.R. organization.

Similar cross references can be set up on regular intervals with I.T. and Real Estate (Property Management) departments to catch discrepancies and fill in information gaps. The key here is to put ongoing processes in place to catch issues while the corrections are still in relatively small batches that are easy to stay on top of.

 **Manually collecting and filling in blank information on the front end prevents a cascade of repeated inefficiencies throughout the remaining H.R. processes.**

Chapter 4: A Word on H.R. Systems – Workforce Reporting

Data Management and H.R. Software

Even if your H.R. information and processes aren't in one system, that doesn't mean you can't have continuity. In fact, the principles covered in this section may actually be MORE ESSENTIAL if you don't have one integrated H.R. application or platform. Establishing disciplined management of H.R. information helps bridge the gaps attributable to using multiple software applications across processes.

And, for those who do have all H.R. processes running on a single software platform, good data management ensures maximum return on your technology investment. Don't assume that a single platform automatically equates to good data management. In a survey conducted by the Society For Human Resource Management (SHRM), respondents who had recently implemented new H.R. technology were asked to rate their level of satisfaction with the application. Only 28% viewed the investments as having been "very successful" and 68% rated the experience as only being "somewhat successful." (Collison, 2005) Certainly there were many factors that contributed to these results, but it's fair to say that the success of any H.R. technology will only be as good as the data management practices in place.

H.R. Metrics that Matter

What internal client most likely associate with your H.R. systems are the reports available to them. Avoid trying to live beyond your means here. Rather, keep it simple and deliver consistently. Seeing very basic information month-over-month is far more helpful to the organization than having complex analysis that isn't easily attainable or repeatable. Supplying basic but reliable workforce metrics to the organization provides a valuable tool that assists operational leaders with running the business. As ho-hum as it may sound, delivering very well on the basics positions H.R. as a strategic partner with those who run the business!

The problem for many H.R. departments is that their reporting activities (whether executed within the department or by other departments on their own) is rife with duplicity. Each department or process owner claims to need their own slightly varied report version or format. Duplicate tasks - in the form of collecting, parsing and formatting the information – are required to generate multiple versions of nearly identical reports. This varied presentation of the same information becomes a breeding ground for issues with report continuity, which ultimately gets blamed as being the result of bad H.R. data.

Creating a Single Source

So what's the solution to this problem? It's the same principle that was discussed in the previous chapters and a common theme throughout this entire book: SIMPLIFY, STANDARDIZE, and INTEGRATE! Begin by taking an inventory of all known H.R. reports, making a list of the data points required. Use the list to establish a *Raw Data Template* from which all reports (well, almost all) get generated going forward. Even if it requires extra effort to collect the data manually or from multiple systems, it is far more efficient than the redundant activity of individually sourcing data for each report.

Once the *Raw Data Template* is in place, the next step is to consolidate as many of the previously generated reports into a single workforce analysis document. We'll call this the *Workforce Core Report*. While serving as the "master" or "consolidated roll up of pertinent employee data, the *Workforce Core Report* also becomes the source (or parent document) for series of reports based on subsets of information. These may include analysis on subsections of the organization or isolating specific data elements to be aggregated in more detail. Illustration 4.1 and Illustration 4.2 summarize the right and wrong way to generate reports.

ILLUSTRATION 4.1

Incorrect Report Methodology

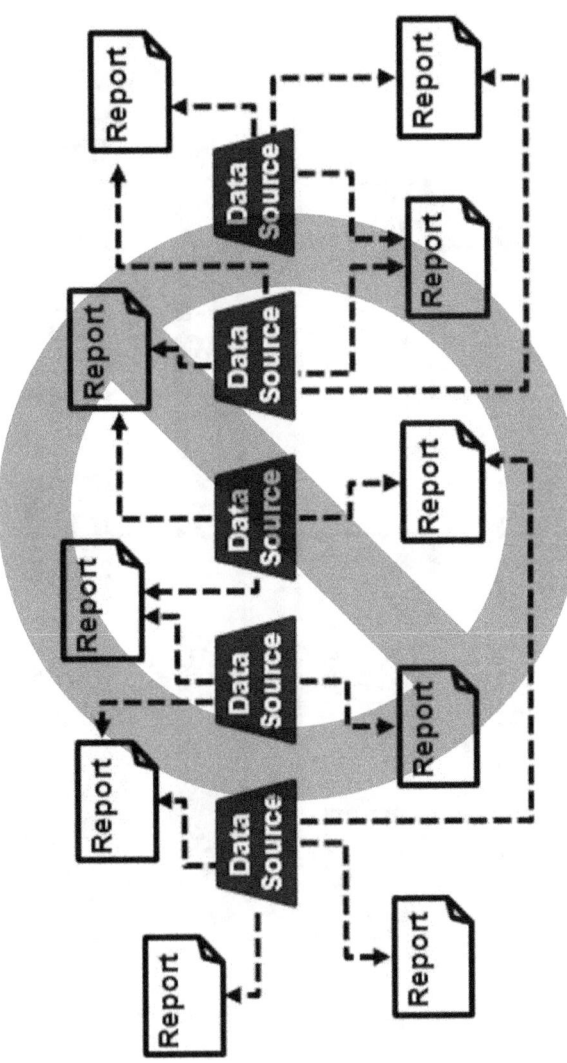

ILLUSTRATION 4.2

Correct Report Methodology

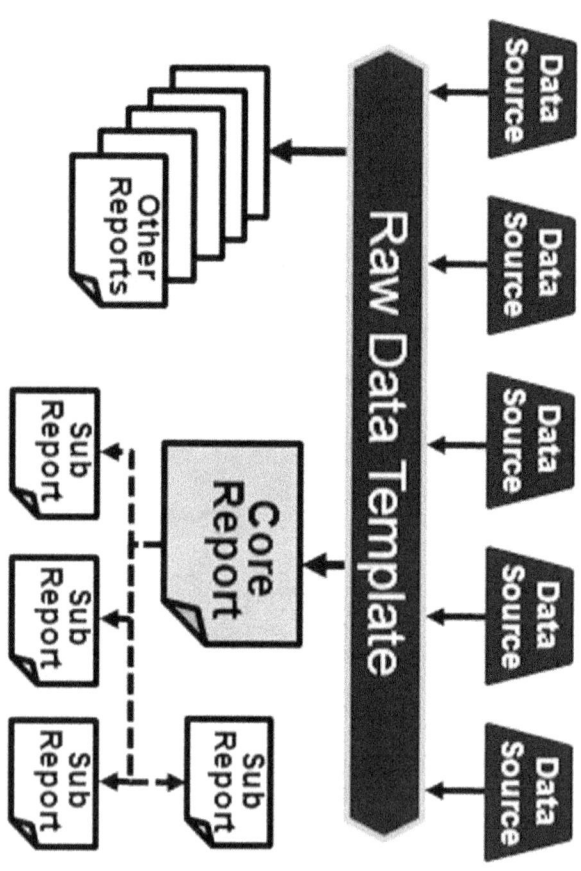

What to Report

As you analyze your past and future reporting needs, the *Workforce Core Report* is likely to take shape as some form of *Employee Demographic Scorecard*. These types of reports serve as a comprehensive snapshot of the organization on a rolling month-over-month, and even year over year basis. Metrics to measure may include total headcount by race, gender, function and organizational hierarchy. If your data definitions allow, consider aggregating the data by level (i.e. management, executive, non-management, etc.) as well. Use the 3-Tier format as the basic framework for presenting this information.

Keep track of the reports by developing a *Standard H.R. Reports Catalog* and applying cascading number sequence to the subsets of information. Illustration 4.3 provides a basic example of how the *Schema* for a *Standard H.R. Reports Catalog* could be designed.

ILLUSTRATION 4.3

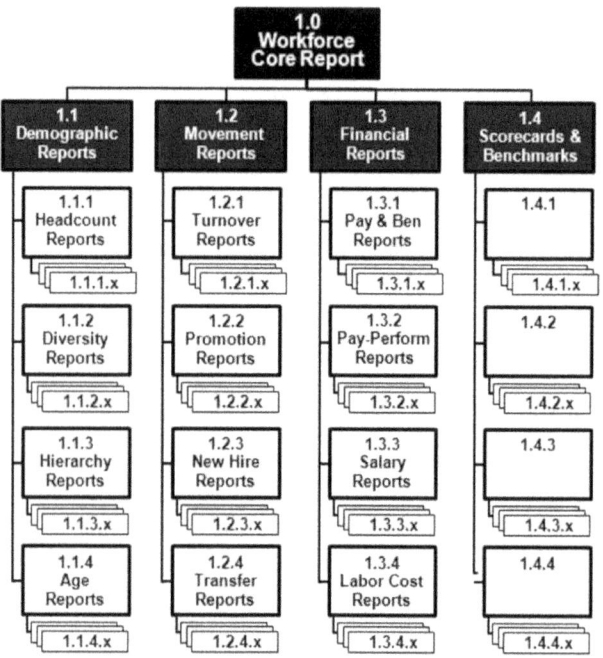

Stick To Your Guns!

Like any other effort to standardize a process, moving many report viewers/users onto one standard format won't be easy. You'll hear hundreds of fascinating stories of why it is "absolutely essential" for certain individuals to have the information presented "their" way. But, the newfound consistency and reliability that will follow conversion to a *Standard H.R. Report Catalog* is almost certain to outweigh their loss of formatting preferences and report names. Taking some time to compile/document the duplicate (and redundant) work that went in to the previously used reports may be an effective way to sell in the standardization to a Single *Workforce Demographics Scorecard*.

Finally, when facing custom report requests, always begin by reviewing the *Standard H.R. Reports Catalog* with the requestor. Continually reinforce -both within H.R. and with other departments - that report requests ALWAYS start with assessing the usability of information from the established reports before custom work can be initiated.

 **More often than not, "Custom" reports are exercises in wastefulness and represent personal preference more than real business need.**

Section II:

Let's Get Integrated!
Moving From Functional Excellence to Seamless Perfection!

Section Introduction: All (H.R.) Roads Lead To This Intersection!

Do your Organizational Development, Compensation and Recruiting department draw upon the same data set when conducting their processes? Let's be a bit more specific. Does your company use the exact same criteria for conducting an employee's performance appraisal/review as they use to evaluate talent inventories and succession plans? Is this the same terminology the Compensation department used to originally price/grade the job? What about recruiting? How closely do the qualities evaluated during the employee's review match the requirements outlined in the job description and job posting used by the Recruiting department?

If you answered "no" to any of these questions, then chances are your H.R. department lacks the integration necessary to ensure continuity and weed out inefficiency.

Applying the adage that: *"A picture's worth a thousand words"*, which of these illustrations most closely represent your organization's level of H.R. integration?

ILLUSTRATION i.1

ILLUSTRATION i.2

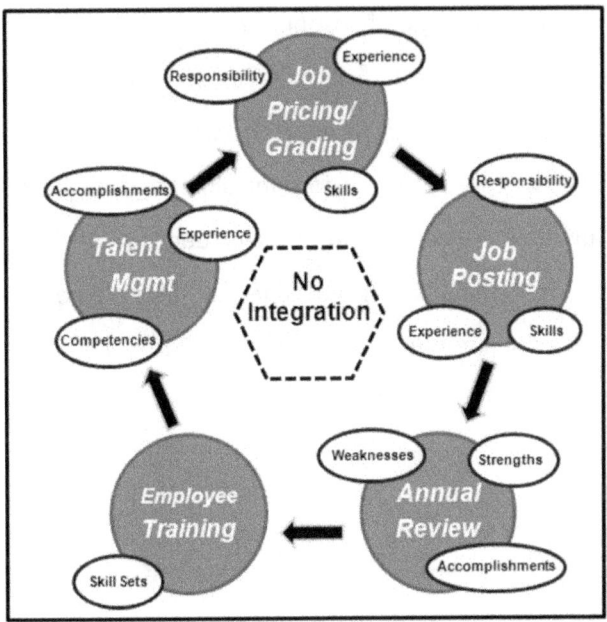

In the following chapters we'll examine what gaps and inconsistencies cause processes to be like Illustration i.2. We'll also outline what can be done to transform your H.R. processes to more closely align with Illustration i.1.

As you read through the ideas and suggestions that follow, it may be tempting to view some of the concepts as being too basic or not cutting edge enough.

But remember that it is the successful and efficient execution of basic deliverables that vaults Human Resource organizations to the next level. The great American writer and philosopher Henry David Thoreau may have said it best: *"...For the Hero is commonly the simplest and obscurest of men [and women]."* (Thoreau) Such is the case with transforming almost any department or function. Any effort put towards seemingly loftier ambitions will be compromised if the basics are not executed in and integrated and efficient manner.

 **The greatest gains come in the efficient execution of a department's most basic processes.**

Chapter 5: Forget About Competency Models

The High Cost of Competency Models

Competency modeling has been a trendy endeavor in H.R. circles for some time now. Many embark on that long road of analyzing, defining and then validating the critical success factors for the jobs in their organization. Some reach the point of deploying a detailed competency model for selected functional disciplines or job families (i.e. sales, customer service, accounting, etc.). Far fewer are the number of companies that reach the point of achieving detailed competency models for ALL areas within the organization. Because true competency models take so much time and resources to create, such undertakings often stall out before reaching completion across all jobs. Perhaps the partially completed task is rationalized by the notion that detailed competencies only need to be identified for the most essential roles. But it is this sort of thinking that fuels the unraveling of integration across H.R. processes.

Still other organizations elect to develop a model that targets companywide leadership competencies rather than complete functional requirements for a given group of jobs. While this may have broader use than the former, it too poses limitations when it comes to helping integrate and optimize all Human Resources activity.

Some seasoned H.R. Professionals are now beginning to question the return on the huge investment that comes with developing both leadership and functional competency models. *"There's no way that you can pick eight competencies (for example) that completely describe the perfect manager. Instead, it's about living a set of core values and then selecting the skills for that particular managerial role,"* says Scott Mannis, who leads the Human Resources function at Kellwood Corporation.

For sure, H.R. leaders face a bit of conundrum on this topic. A full blown competency model has the capability to do amazing things, yet it can be costly and is certainly quite time consuming to deploy. Further compounding the decision is the backlog of more immediate needs for applying limited resources and funds. And, of course, a thing like competency model development typically doesn't play well with operational leaders who are screaming for better H.R. performance RIGHT NOW!

However, there is a practical alternative to competency models and it's a relatively quick solution. Consider a basic proficiency catalog instead. It's less painful to develop, easier to deploy across H.R. functional silos, and simpler to maintain. Plus, a proficiency catalog can help establish cross-functional standardization of H.R. nomenclature and qualifications for areas not typically included in a competency model. Before we delve into the specifics of creating a proficiency catalog, let's take a further look at the integration gaps across H.R. functions as they relate to qualifications.

Just How Big Is The Problem?

How many sets of qualifications (be it formal or informal) does your company have for a given job? I'll bet that most organizations – even those with defined competency models - maintain multiple sets of qualifications for any given job. As an example, let's examine the all too typical lifecycle of a job as it relates to the use of qualifications.

When a new job is approved, some combination involving the H.R. Rep and hiring manager create the initial job description. The Compensation department uses this to market price the salary and to apply internal grading systems that may be in place. This becomes the **FIRST** set of qualifications.

Sometime within the first year, the hiring manager conducts the *Annual Review* or performance appraisal. Chances are, the criteria used to evaluate the employee's performance will not be completely identical to what was used to initially define the job. This represents the **SECOND** set of qualifications used and maintained for this job.

If the organization conducts some sort of talent management activity, such as succession planning or, leadership development, the O.D. function typically applies its own variation of qualities, conditions and attributes to complete their assessment. That makes the **THIRD** set of qualifications used to manage human capital relating to this position.

Finally, at some point, the position in this example becomes vacant. So the Recruiting department works with the hiring manager to create a job posting. Perhaps there's a new manager since the position was originally created. Or, maybe there are multiple people in this same position across more than one manager and/or department. In either case, it's likely that the job posting will highlight still other experience, skills or attributes. Thus, the **FOURTH** set of qualifications.   Now, multiply this by all job titles and level of inefficiency can be tremendous.   The result is an overall H.R. process map like the one depicted back in Illustration i.2.

This is precisely how integration across H.R. functional areas unravels. Each area of H.R. seeks perfection for their given process. It's all very well meaning. Compensation wants a job description crafted in a manner that helps them best price and slot the job. The O.D. function strives to evaluate talent using criteria that maximizes organizational potential. Recruiting seeks to pull in the very best candidates for each hiring manager's current needs. But, when cohesiveness is lost, the integration across H.R. processes (as well as within each given process) begins to splinter. This leads to the inefficiency and slow process cycles that cause internal clients to shake their heads in disgust when they hear the words HUMAN RESOURCES.

Here are just a few examples of how the fragmented application of qualifications can impact the speed and quality of H.R. operations:

1. Requisitioning & Job Pricing: It's really quite simple. The more sets of qualifications (either formal or informal), the more job titles get proliferated. The more job titles, the more workload and administration placed on the Compensation department which then further slows the approval process for new jobs, promotions, etc.

2. *Performance Appraisals*: Few things are more despised by managers than hitting company mandated deadlines for this task.   A good amount of the duplicate assessment and rehashing of information can be avoided if there is process and criteria alignment between annual reviews and talent management activities. But that sort of continuity is not feasible when separate sets of qualifications are used across each process.

3. Recruiting & Hiring: The amount of time spent recreating and re-handling job postings &

descriptions could be redirected to primary recruiting activities that reduce overall time-to-fill metrics for openings across the organization.

- <u>H.R. Generalist Transactions:</u> Oh the administrative work! Do we really need to say anything more about this one?

Moving to a Solution

The faster-easier-cheaper alternative to competency modeling is to create a simple proficiency catalog. It is similar to a competency model in that it is comprised of various groupings of skills, abilities and other qualities used to define roles in the organization. However, a proficiency catalog does not have the complexity and granularity by position that makes competency models so difficult to create and maintain. And, because the criteria are a bit more generic, it stands to reason that there would typically be fewer legal issues around validation as well.

In its simplest form, the proficiency catalog is a collection of common nomenclature used throughout H.R. to evaluate and categorize people and positions/roles. When all H.R. functions are drawing from this same set of standardized terms, the continuity across processes and data immediately become more standardized. H.R. as an operation becomes simpler and clearer. As this happens, the ability to execute on more advanced Human Resources functions increases exponentially. This occurs because:

1) High end initiatives are integrated with, and therefore reinforced, by daily H.R. transactions, and

2) More advanced activities become less complicated since they are built on a foundation of process integration.

Remember, more sophisticated does not mean "better".   It's hard to imagine that something this basic can make things run so much smoother – but that's exactly the point of this book!

Getting Started

It's quite possible that the contents of an organization's basic proficiency catalog is already assembled (albeit informally and unformatted) throughout existing H.R. forms. Such documents include job descriptions, applicant forms, performance appraisal documents, compensation analysis templates, and various talent management instruments.

Begin by collecting all these documents and taking an inventory of what gets "rated" or "measured" when it comes to positions and employees. Think in broad terms across all H.R. activities. What we're trying to do is look for opportunities to establish standard measurements across all H.R. procedures and transactions. For example, *Years of Experience* is a data point that gets used on job descriptions, applications, and numerous talent management activities. Yet it's very common for an organization to use a different "scale" to measure *Years of Experience* on each of the processes referenced in Table 5.1.

TABLE 5.1

Example: Using Multiple "Experience" Ratings		
Compensation	Recruiting	Talent Mgmt
No Exp	Less Than 1 Year	Under 1 year
1 Year	1-3 Years	1-2 Years
2 Years	4-5 Years	3-4 Years
3 Years	5-10 Years	5-7 Years
4 Years...	10+ Years	7-10 Years

Here are a few more opportunities that might be ripe for establishing uniformity of measurement/terms across processes:

- Education: Standardizing the format (degree, major, institution, dates) on applications, resumes and talent management instruments.

- Skills & Attributes: Utilizing the same terms and selection criteria on job descriptions, performance appraisals and talent management documents. We'll examine this category in more detail in a moment.

- Performance Ratings: Performance management and talent management processes become more seamless and the data more transferrable (less duplicative) when both processes are standardized on the same ratings.

- Language Skills: When both the list of languages and the fluency ratings are standardized, then information collected during the applicant and selection processes can be immediately plugged-in to talent management activities.

- Willingness/Ability to Relocate: This data point often appears on applications, job postings and can surface during the analysis that occurs during career and succession planning.

- <u>Expertise:</u> A standard scale for level of expertise can be deployed regardless of the skill, ability or experience being rated.

When you begin using the same terms and data structures across H.R. functions, then processes automatically start "feeding" information to each other. As a result, administrative tasks are diminished, processes become more seamless, and the H.R. function slowly elevates itself to those much pursued high profile activities.

The following tables are examples of how your proficiency catalog might look at this point. Again, these are only examples. Your categories and ratings formats may differ. What's most important is to make sure that the terms/scales selected are used consistently across all H.R. activities.

TABLES 5.2

Ratings & Scales		
Performance	**Experience**	**Relocation**
High Performer	Less Than 1 Year	No Restrictions
Strong Performer	1-3 Years	Within Country
Meets Requirements	4-5 Years	Within State/Region
Under Performing	5-10 Years	Local
Action Required	10+ Years	Temporarily Restricted

TABLE 5.3

Education			
Degree	**Major**	**Institution**	**Year**
Coursework	H.R.	Univ. Of Missouri	1995
Certificate	Engineering	UCLA	1996
Associates	Accounting	St. Louis Univ.	1997
Bachelors	Education	Fontbonne Univ.	1998
Grad. Courses	Business	Univ. Of Illinois	1999
Masters	Biology	Northwestern	2000
MBA	I.T.	STL Comm College	2001
J.D.	Psych.	Silver View Tech.	2002
PhD	History	Columbia	2003
Other	*More...*	*More...*	*More.*

TABLE 5.4

Language *Ratings*	
Vernacular	**Proficiency**
English	Beginner
Spanish	Intermediate
German	Fluent
French	Culturally Advanced
More...	

Once the most obvious categories are identified, make a first attempt at constructing lists like the examples previously shown in Tables 5.2 – 5.4. The next step is to conduct initial reviews with all stakeholders. Remember to use the data owners (identified in Chapter 3) to help establish buy-in and drive towards firm decisions.

The *Scales & Ratings* portion of the proficiency catalog is the quickest to define. The next section to develop is the *Expertise* component. While this may require a bit more consideration, it should still demand considerably fewer resources and time than what goes into developing a series of competency models.

One approach to developing *Expertise* section is to simply purchase a generic list from a consulting service and then customize as needed. Many are readily available and can be found through a simple internet search. Some companies, professional organizations and even governmental entities even make their catalogs available to the public. Seeing what other entities are using can be an excellent point of reference for creating your own catalog.

Yet another avenue is to gather all of the performance appraisals from the most recent review cycle and then compile a list of all the strengths and weaknesses (sometimes referred to as development needs) identified across the entire workforce. Analyze the list to remove duplicate terms and condense like qualities into a one common term. Since EVERY process (job pricing, recruiting, annual reviews/appraisals, talent inventories & succession planning and employee development/training, etc.) will utilize the same terms, it is important to include all the necessary stakeholders early on to get buy-in on one standardized – and hopefully simplified – list. This may be a bit of a challenge at first, as various H.R. functions plead their case for unique wording and descriptors they feel are essential. But, resist such temptations by appealing to the greater good that comes from continuity and simplicity. Sticking to this principle now pays big dividends for the entire H.R. operation later!

For some, it is helpful to break the list into separate groupings for *Skills*, *Attributes* and *Functional Knowledge*. Any trait that is technical in nature and/or describes an activity or task is usually considered a "Skill". Conversely, *Attributes* are normally those items that describe a quality or trait an employee possesses. For some industries, "physical skills" are an important requirement noted on job descriptions and job postings. Such abilities might include tasks like walking, lifting, repetitive motions, etc. Including a list of physical requirements as part of the overall skills list is one method to help ensure regulatory compliance.

There aren't perfectly defined parameters as to how many *Skills and Attributes* should be included in a proficiency catalog. Certainly the correct amount varies by organization. However, a very general guideline is to be cautious about having a list that exceeds 50-75 skills and/or attributes. This suggestion is based more on personal experience around ease of management than on any formal research or benchmarking. Remember, the bottom line is to keep everything as practical as possible.

Table 5.5

Expertise	
Skills	**Attributes**
Accounting Principles	Analytical Thinking
Interviewing Skills	Holistic Thinking
Selling Skills	Process Oriented
Contract Negotiations	Time Management
Labor Relations	Multi Tasking
	Flexibility
More...	More...

The last portion of the proficiency catalog is the list of *Functional Expertise*. One way to establish the criteria for *Functional Expertise* is to think of this list as being similar to the career or professional paths used to categorize job titles. Another method might be to think of it as being closely aligned with the primary functions that make up your business. If you've already aligned and simplified the company's organizational data (as described in Chapter 2), then this task may already be in the final phase of completion. This is a critical integration point in that, the data used/generated for both recruiting and talent management activities then aligns perfectly with your organizational tiers, thus making H.R. Reporting & Analysis much cleaner.

TABLE 5.6

Functional Knowledge	
Accounting	Customer Service
Procurement	Sales
Human Resources	Marketing
Finance	Warehouse & Distribution
Manufacturing/Ops.	Administrative
Legal	Real Estate / Property Mgmt
Communications	R&D
Regulatory	*More...*

The integration value of having all H.R. activities standardized on the proficiency catalog cannot be over emphasized. Individual processes and functions may sacrifice some flexibility – though very minimal. However, the dividends realized through eliminating duplicity and improved continuity will outweigh any takeaways. You'll be able to readily use existing information generated from other processes, and your internal clients will be less confused by the standardization of terms.

Illustration 5.2 depicts the structure of the proficiency catalog, based on the example used in this chapter. It's less important whether you elect to follow this example or adopt a different *Schema*. What is essential is that one set of common terms become the standard nomenclature for ALL Human Resources activities so that information can be leveraged across ALL processes. The remainder of this book contains additional detail on how each H.R. function can apply and benefit from using a proficiency catalog.

 **To be fully integrated and optimized, all H.R. Functions must operate from one COMMON and SIMPLE set of ratings, scales and proficiencies.**

ILLUSTRATION 5.2

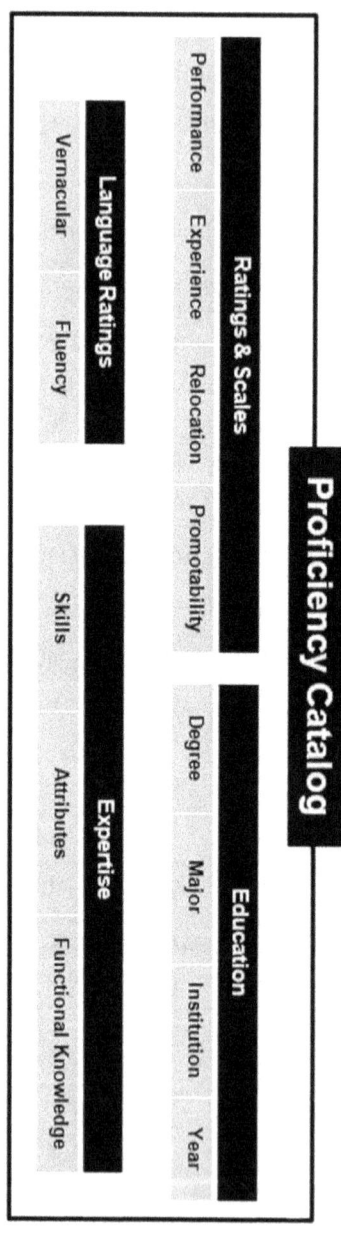

Chapter 6: Job Definitions

Job Descriptions Vs. Job Definitions and Roles

How many pages are your company's job descriptions? How up-to-date are they? How many are missing and/or redundant? Do you handle and generate both a job description and a separate job posting document every time a position comes open? The degree to which you answer these questions will be directly proportional to how much waste is embedded in your H.R. process and consequently how happy your internal clients are with the overall H.R. function.

Job descriptions epitomize the gap that is the underlying theme of this book. It's something that many organizations don't do a good job managing. As H.R. Director Steve Malec admits, "Every single organization I've been with, maintaining job descriptions has always been a struggle... It's (always) one of those projects we need to do eventually."

Too often, H.R. leaders view them as only a "nice to have", or else a low priority because they are not looked at as "strategic" work. This is unfortunate because it's exactly these basic foundations that, when in place, streamline and integrate processes in a manner that allow H.R. Resources to then truly focus on the strategic work they are so passionately seeking to do. According to Malec, "Having adequate job descriptions is essential for effective labor relations, especially when it comes to issues surrounding job bidding, ADA and other areas of regulatory compliance."

The key here is to keep foundational components like job descriptions as practical and low maintenance as possible. One approach is to opt for a *job definition* rather than the conventional "job description". The former is a concise, one page version that combines a broad swatch across many job titles. (See Illustration 6.1) What's the benefit? Well, my research suggests that it's not uncommon for large companies to have over 3,000 job titles. Now, what organization could possibly accurately maintain and keep track of 3,000 job descriptions? How does that relate to the length of a job description document you might ask? Well, the more pages and sections of intricate detail held in the document, the more both H.R. and hiring managers are apt to differentiate similar jobs — usually far beyond what is really necessary.

But, if the company were to opt for a simple one-page *job definition*, with each serving as an umbrella for multiple roles, then the list of 3,000 job descriptions is reduced down to as little as a few hundred. That's a volume that would be manageable to conduct an annual H.R. event in which hiring managers are asked to do a quick review/update of the *job definition*s. This ultimately saves the hiring manager time in the long run as future openings occur and annual reviews are conducted. BUT, asking them to review 3,000 multi-page job descriptions on an annual basis is the very thing that would have them howling about the ineffectiveness of the H.R. department.

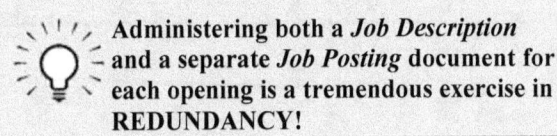 Administering both a *Job Description* and a separate *Job Posting* document for each opening is a tremendous exercise in **REDUNDANCY!**

ILLUSTRATION 6.1

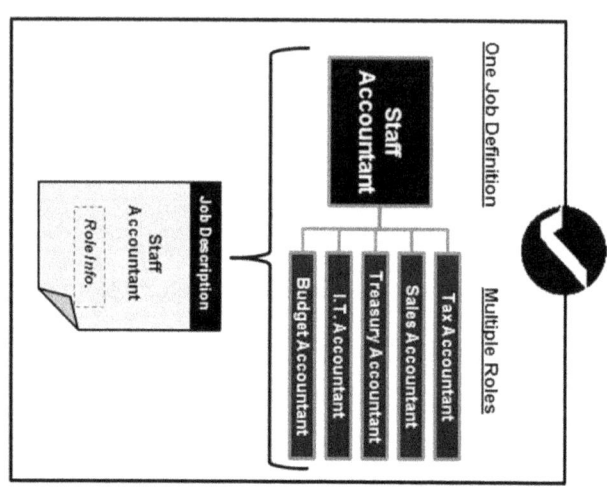

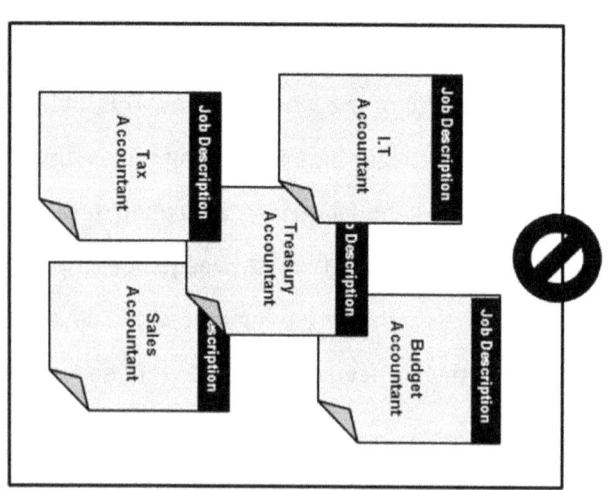

Continuity of Titles, Departments, Etc.

In an effort to be customer focused, often times H.R. reps are their own worst enemy when it comes to the proliferation of job titles. Hiring managers (and sometimes even the hired employee themselves) seek tweaks to job titles already held by other employees. This results in the creation of yet another job title and description document – thus exacerbating the problem by creating yet another job description that needs to be maintained.

So, while utilizing a *job definition/role* format for your documents is an essential component to integrating and streamlining H.R. processes, equally important is for the organization to demonstrate discipline around the creation and proliferation of job titles. Being able to say "No" is a must when hiring managers begin demanding a new or "customized" job title. Of course it is incumbent upon the H.R. professional to do so in a manner that helps the hiring manager understand why it's in their best interest in the long run to rationalize job titles (and consequently *job definitions*).

Keep in mind that, while managers may not value this exercise in discipline at that very moment, they'll be more than grateful when other workforce events occur throughout the year. The more job titles an organization has, the more cumbersome activities like salary/budget planning, performance management, succession planning and organizational reporting (a.k.a. org charts) will be. Even filling out forms for basic employee transactions takes more time and is more error prone when the list of titles grows longer.

 **The more job titles a company has, the longer it takes to process H.R. transactions, forms become more complicated, and error rates increase.**

ILLUSTRATION 6.2

THE PROLIFERATION OF JOB TITLES...

Components of the One-Page Job Definition

Illustration 6.3 is a sample of a basic *Job definition*. It is comprised of the three following sections:

1 Basic_Information: Title, Pay/Grade, Summary Description and details regarding the current opening.

2 Responsibilities: The 1-5 primary tasks that comprise the job, a description of the specific "role" associated with the current opening, other roles that also fall under this *job definition*, and the functional knowledge required.

3 Qualifications: The education, experience and skills/attributes assigned to this *job definition*.

The individual data points that make up each of these sections may vary by company, depending on industry, regulatory requirements, and type of H.R. technology in use.

ILLUSTRATION 6.3

SAMPLE JOB DEFINITION DOCUMENT

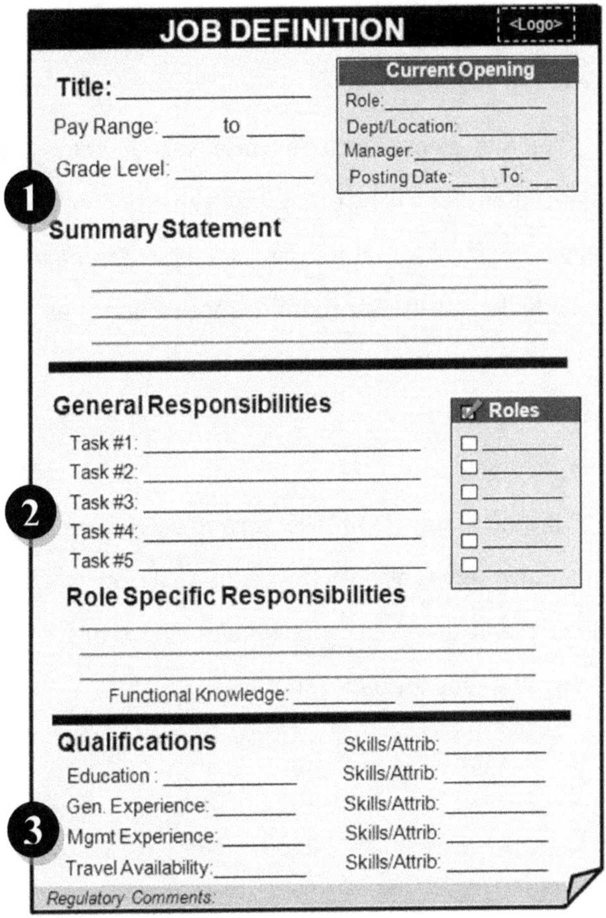

It's important that the options in the qualifications fields are identical to what is listed in your proficiency catalog (This includes the role specific

Functional Knowledge field in the General Responsibilities section). If possible, create the *job definition* document in a spreadsheet or eForm so drop-down menus limit input to lists from the proficiency catalog.

You may elect to include a brief section at the end of the document for calling out notable environmental and regulatory factors that pertain to the job. Examples may include: heavy lifting, repetitive motion activities, high stress, or any other occupational health circumstances that apply.

If the *Job definition* is set up and used correctly, then one form serves as both the traditional "job description" and "job posting". This alone becomes a time saver and reduces paper shuffling.

Chapter 7: Using The Proficiency Catalog

Recruiting

If you work for a manufacturing company, chances are the production environment has some form of scrap recovery or recycling program to reduce and re-use purchased materials/supplies. Now, think of the recruiting process as a procurement exercise to acquire candidates. But how well does your recruiting function recycle and re-use its purchased "materials/supplies" to reduce waste?

Finding candidates can be costly. When commissions are paid to external recruiters, fees to job boards or advertisements purchased, you are essentially buying resumes. From an H.R. standpoint these are the cost of materials or supplies. The way to keep costs down for recruiting is to "recycle" the unused materials/supplies (i.e. resumes), similar to the way manufacturing operations implement *Recapture and Re-Use* programs to prevent waste.

So, how does waste occur in the recruiting process? Money is paid, an array of resumes are received. A few are selected for evaluation and then the vast majority of the remaining  resumes are more or less thrown away. It's a fair argument that, unless an organization has invested in a resume management application, it is far too cumbersome to manually hold onto the resumes for future openings in other areas.

This is where the proficiency catalog can help ease the burden – especially for those organizations that do not have electronic recruiting or resume management technologies. If you've used the proficiency catalog to simplify and align roles to *Job definition*s (as described in Chapter 5), then mapping jobs with similar qualifications is a fairly straightforward exercise. Using a spreadsheet, list all the Job title in your organization on the left side of the document. Each column that follows to the right represents a qualification contained in the proficiency catalog. Simply identify the position for which candidates are being sought and sort the contents of the spreadsheet to locate the jobs with similar requirements. Finally, pull the resumes and/or applications for the most recent openings within the jobs that have similar requirements. Of course it's important to augment the "recycled" resumes/applications with fresh candidates to keep the resource pool current, and to comply with regulatory requirements. However, re-using even a small percentage of resumes/applications can result in a cost savings with very limited time investment.

Figure 7.1 provides a sample of how a spreadsheet might look for cross-referencing jobs with similar proficiencies for the purpose of re-using recently acquired resumes.

ILLUSTRATION 7.1

	A	B	C	D	E	F	G	H
1	Position	General Experience	Management Experience	Functional Knowledge	Functional Knowledge	Skills & Attributes	Skills & Attributes	Skills & Attributes
2	Production Supervisor	4-5 yrs	1-2 yrs	Manufacturing	Engineering	Supervisory Skills	Technical	Organization
3	Accountant II	1-3 yrs	-	Accounting	Finance	Analytical Skills	Organization	Detail Oriented
4	Sales Analyst	1-3 yrs	-	Accounting	Sales	Analytical Skills	Selling Skills	Presentation Skills
5	Cost Administrator	1-3 yrs	-	Accounting	Accounts Payable	Organization	Analytical Skills	Detail Oriented
6	Project Coordinator	1-3 yrs	-	Accounting	Project Mgmt.	Analytical Skills	Collaboration	Flexibility
7	Customer Svc Rep II	0-1 yrs	-	Service	Sales	Communication	Flexibility	Interpersonal

For organizations that already have a resume management application or database in place, then much of what is described in the previous paragraphs can already be done electronically. Still, there is value in configuring the software to align with the proficiency catalog. Not only does this continue the integration and standardization, but it also may help maximize the return on your technology investment. Two common complaints about many resume management and recruiting software are that they are cumbersome to use and yield mixed search results. Once again, the simplification and standardization of the proficiency catalog can help reduce these types of application issues.

The final component for integrating the recruiting function via the proficiency catalog pertains to structured interviews. Similar to how organizations utilize a competency model, work to establish standardized sets of questions for each qualification included in the proficiency catalog. Remember, the underlying theme is to SIMPLIFY – STANDARDIZE – INTEGRATE. So, the goal here is to use the same interview questions for a given proficiency regardless of the role, rather than managing/maintaining unique interview questions for each job title.

Illustration 7.2 is an attempt to capture a few of the inefficiencies throughout the recruiting function that can be minimized by deploying a proficiency catalog.

ILLUSTRATION 7.2

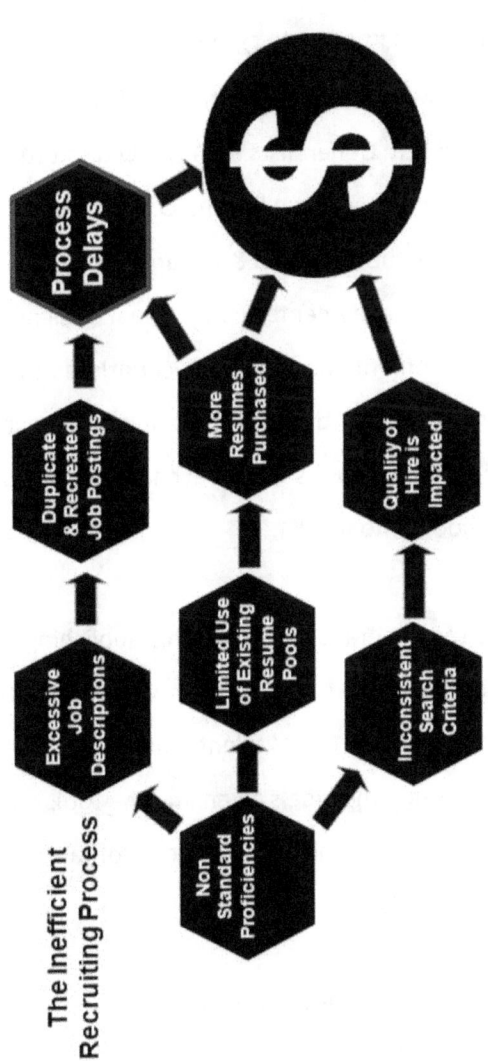

Nowhere is the integration gap more prevalent than the gorge that frequently separates O.D. from the rest of Human Resources – NOT THAT THE ORGANIZATIONAL DEVELOPMENT DEPARTMENT IS SOLELY TO BLAME FOR THIS! On the contrary, it's astonishing how many Compensation professionals, Recruiters and H.R. Generalists admittedly don't really know (or care) much about what the O.D. group really does. Of course, the Industrial & Organizational Psychologists, Change Agents, Instructional Designers, Process Improvement Specialists and countless other titles that gather under the O.D. "umbrella", share in perpetuating these gaps as well. But that's a topic worthy of another book unto itself.

For the general purposes of this publishing, and specifically this portion of the chapter, we'll focus our attention on a few Key O.D. / talent management processes. Though the labels given and the tools used may vary by company, the basic elements of talent management involve:

1) Assessing workforce capabilities and requirements

2) Maintaining inventories of human assets

3) Establishing succession/workforce plans (This includes employee development which is discussed in Chapter 9).

Of these activities, H.R. professionals outside of the O.D. function are most familiar with the succession planning component. The problem is that the talent assessment or talent inventory process that is a prerequisite to succession planning is a data intensive process. Effective succession plans can't be developed without first taking a detailed inventory of what abilities exist in the organization.

Talent management is a perfect example of how H.R. can be its own worst enemy. Our profession tends to reward complexity as being synonymous with effectiveness. Intricate competency models for each functional group (i.e. Sales, Accounting, Marketing, Manufacturing, etc.) may be great for a specific O.D. task, but are of limited overall value if they take years to develop and aren't easily adaptable for use to ALL H.R. processes.

Perhaps Anne Offner PhD, owner of Offner & Associates (an H.R. consulting Firm) sums it up best. *"Supply Chain is expected to have end-to-end process unity, why shouldn't H.R. be required to have the same consistency?"* Offner specifically cites the frequency with which processes are administered largely by one H.R. function, but ownership is claimed by another. For example, she has observed that the O.D. function usually teaches the principles of performance management, but the Compensation department is typically the owner and gatekeeper of the process parameters. If these two departments aren't highly integrated, then overall effectiveness is almost certain to be diminished.

The fact is, you can't have great O.D. output and a poor Compensation group. Nor can you sustain a terrific recruiting function while having performance management processes that are subpar. That's why it's so important that O.D. processes are developed with the practicality that allows for application across all of Human Resources. What's more, there is data readily available throughout H.R. that, if formatted correctly, can help talent management initiatives run more effectively.

Unfortunately, few companies take advantage of these opportunities. Studies indicate that less than 10% of organizations consider their talent & succession processes to be automated and integrated, with about one-third rating succession activities as being only partially automated and nearly two-thirds relying entirely on paper based activities. (Succession Planning Benchmarking Report)

ILLUSTRATION 7.3
TECHNOLOGY

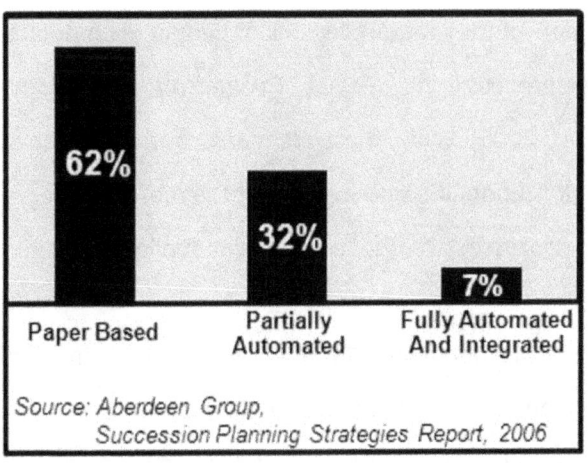

This lack of integration between O.D. and the rest of H.R. makes the talent inventory process far more cumbersome than it needs to be. For example, how long does it take your organization to complete its annual talent assessment activities and then develop succession plans? Once completed, how frequently is it used to help make resource decisions?   Does the succession plan become quickly outdated? And, if so, how much work goes into keeping it up to date? Talent management processes are of limited value if they only get dusted off and looked at once a year. (Fegley, *Succession Planning* Survey Report, 2006)

Similarly, it's difficult for talent management efforts to become part of the institutional fabric of the company if they require legions of people to complete a single process cycle. (Fegley, *Talent Management* Survey Report, 2006). While there are many contributors to such low utilization, it's safe to say that the more cumbersome such processes are, the less they get applied.

I've personally observed organizations in which the talent inventory phase alone takes 4-5 months. A basic proficiency catalog that is integrated across recruiting and performance management can cut the amount of time by at least 50%. If these conditions sound familiar, (or perhaps you are not even able to complete a talent assessment at all), then your organization will almost certainly benefit from the simplification that comes with deploying a proficiency catalog.

Illustration 7.4 provides a quick glance at the inefficiencies that arise when there is limited integration across O.D. processes and throughout the larger H.R. function.

 **The vast majority of Talent Management processes are conducted manually, with little or no integration.**

ILLUSTRATION 7.4

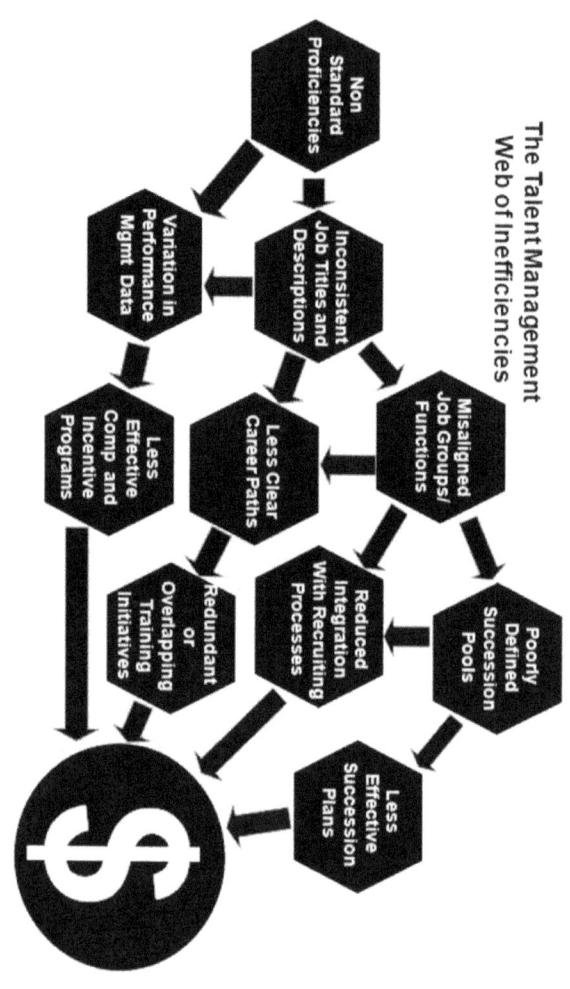

The Talent Management
Web of Inefficiencies

So let's begin by applying the principle discussed in Chapter 1 that information or data is what drives all H.R. processes. In the case of performing talent inventories, the data needed is generated from recruiting, employee lifecycle transactions associated with everyday Generalist functions and performance management activities regulated by Compensation Policies. As we just discussed, the talent inventory activity serves as a means to organize and asses the data so that the necessary information is available to make quality succession planning decisions. These decisions then serve as new information to better drive the other H.R. processes outside of O.D. (See Illustration 7.5). When this occurs, the benefits of process integration begin to emerge and in fact become self-perpetuating. Whether this is a relatively seamless process where H.R. functions further enable one another, versus a manually intensive effort, depends largely on the level of data continuity across all H.R. processes. Once again, the proficiency catalog comes into play!

To perform the talent inventory, start by creating a *talent bio* for each employee. This document gets sent to each employee's manager for review and further completion. The goal is to supply a *talent bio* on each employee (in the identified talent pool), with as many of the data points as possible pre-populated. Such a task becomes far less administrative if the data management principles covered in Section I are in place.

 **When O.D. Functions operate in a vacuum or in an arena separate from the rest of HR, then its own processes become less efficient and effective.**

ILLUSTRATION 7.5

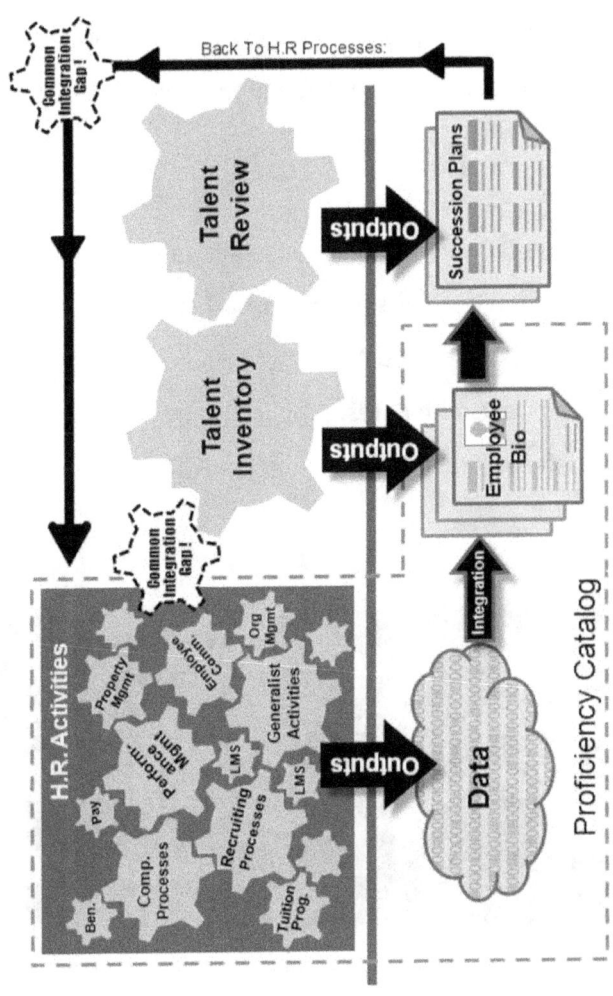

Illustration 7.6 offers an example of a basic *talent bio* that can be used to conduct talent inventories. The key is to develop a talent inventory and review/assessment process that leverages the readily available information generated across other H.R. functions which also use the shared proficiency catalog.

Some O.D. professionals and even organizational leaders may view this sort of approach as being too basic. However, as renowned Author and H.R. Consultant Marshall Goldsmith notes, simplicity is the key to successful sustainable succession plan. (Goldsmith, 2009)

> *If you cannot do great things, do small things in a great way.*
>
> **Napoleon Hill**

ILLUSTRATION 7.6

TALENT BIO

<Logo>

CORE INFORMATION

Name: _____   Gender: _____
Title: _____   Race: _____
Dept: _____   Function: _____
Hire Date: _____   Grade/Level: ____

Photo

EXPERIENCE

Internal Job	Yr.	External Job/Co.	Yr.
_____	__	_____	__
_____	__	_____	__

TRAINING

Program	Yr.
_____	__
_____	__

EDUCATION

Degree	Major	Institute	Year
_____	_____	_____	_____
_____	_____	_____	_____

PERFORMANCE

Current Year Rating: _____
Prior Year Rating: _____

Key Accomplishments
_____
_____
_____

PROFICIENCIES

Skill/Attribute/Function

Gen. Experience: ____ yrs.   Expertise: _____
Mgmt Experience: ___ yrs.   Expertise: _____
Language #1: _____   Expertise: _____
Language #2: _____   Expertise: _____
Geo/Travel Restrictions: _____   Expertise: _____

RESOURCE PLANNING

Potential Successors	Career Interests	Probable Paths	Development Needs
_____	_____	_____	_____
_____	_____	_____	_____
_____	_____	_____	_____

Notations/Comments:

Compensation Department as Gatekeeper

If the O.D. function is responsible for determining what proficiencies are important and understanding who possesses them, then it could be said that that the Compensation department owns the process for assigning a value to each group of proficiencies that constitutes a family of jobs.

The document that captures this is of course the *Job definition*. While they are used by Recruiting, Compensation, H.R. Generalists, and even in various O.D. activities, it's surprising how many companies don't have a formal owner of the job description document. Ideally, the generalist role should create the job description; the recruiting function should be the key user; and the Compensation department serves as the gatekeeper/owner. Why? Because every time the core requirements (a.k.a. proficiencies) significantly change for a job, the Compensation department should in theory re-evaluate or re-price that position. If this doesn't happen, then continuity issues progressively surface in titles, compensation and incentive levels and eventually in the quality and accuracy of how succession pools get defined.

When a new job is created and placed in the hands of the Compensation department for market pricing and slotting, they are responsible for ensuring that all identified requirements fit within the selection criteria of the proficiency catalog. Once the job is priced and slotted, the core proficiencies (excluding the role information, which we'll cover in the next chapter) should remain the same each time the job is recruited during subsequent openings. If modifications to a job's proficiencies are required, then this means the job has fundamentally changed, and therefore needs to be re-evaluated. That's why the core proficiencies should only be modified when the job fundamentally changes.

Unfortunately, more often than not, hiring managers insist on modifying this portion of job descriptions/postings each time an opening occurs. H.R. Generalists, Recruiters, and even O.D. professionals all share in the responsibility for being disciplined around the guidelines set forth by the Compensation department. A failure to do so negates the integration benefits of the proficiency catalog and compromises overall data continuity downstream in the employee lifecycle.

Performance Mgmt & Pay-For-Performance

If you've come so far on the integration path as to price jobs, recruit for candidates and evaluate potential successors all based on the same set of proficiencies, it only makes sense to do the same for rating and incenting performance. Whatever the mechanism for conducting annual reviews, the integration cycle is not complete unless the assessments are based on the criteria from the proficiency catalog. Like the other integration practices discussed thus far, using the same criteria for performance management makes data from annual reviews immediately usable during the talent inventory and succession planning processes.

Building the performance management process around the proficiency catalog also creates opportunities for both Compensation and O.D. to perform more meaningful analysis on Pay-For-Performance. Performance incentives become more equitably based on consistent evaluation metrics. Plus, the organization can evaluate patterns in which specific proficiencies appear to be more regarded and whether they are being incented appropriately. This is a frequent gap in many Pay-For-Performance systems. Too often, certain skills are heralded as being vital during recruiting, annual reviews and succession plans, but the pay out of incentive programs doesn't necessarily correlate. The data alignment that occurs when all H.R. processes use the proficiency catalog allows for such analysis to occur.

Chapter 8: Another Word on H.R. Systems

As your data dictionary indicates, there are a number of functions outside Human Resources that rely on the same or at least similar data points as those housed in H.R. systems. Taking a leadership role to synchronize this information benefits H.R. processes, and increases continuity of (and credibility for) employee and organizational data. It also positions H.R. as a companywide process integrator. AND THAT IN ITSELF IS PROVIDING STRATEGIC VALUE TO THE ORGANIZATION!

The following pages are a few examples of areas outside of H.R. in which system and process, integration opportunities may exist.

ILLUSTRATION 8.1

STRATEGIC H.R.: USING EMPLOYEE DATA TO OPTIMIZE NON-H.R. BUSINESS PROCESSES

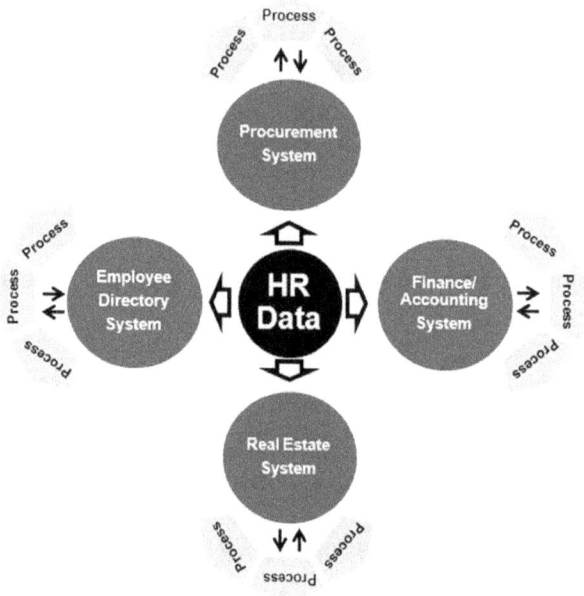

Employee Directories

Perhaps the most used feature on an organization's intranet site is the *Employee Directory*. And usually, the Human Resources department shares in at least some level of accountability for the information housed in the employee directory. A survey on H.R. technology conducted by SHRM validates this point.

When asked which H.R. programs and activities were most frequently supported by H.R. technology systems, 61% of the respondents included employee directories. (Collison, 2005) While some companies place the bulk of the burden on the I.T. department, or perhaps even the employees and departments themselves, it's still essential from both an efficiency and credibility standpoint that H.R. data and the employee directory are in sync.

If employees/departments are responsible for entering and maintaining this information, then it's almost a certainty that things like job titles and department names in the employee directory do not align with what is in H.R. systems. Unfortunately, it's more likely that employees will recognize what the employee directory says over H.R. data. The ensuing data discrepancy bogs down H.R. processes when it comes time to complete forms and conduct transactions.

So, when you begin creating the data dictionary that was described in Section I, be sure to include employee directory information when defining data points such as location, department, job title, etc. The ideal scenario is to have an automated feed from the H.R.

Master Data repository to the employee directory application. If this cannot be attained, then at least make sure that any information manually entered by employees into the employee directory are "fixed input" (i.e. drop down menus) fields which align with the selection criteria used in H.R. systems, forms, etc.

Periodic audits to ensure the employee directory and H.R. systems are aligned is time well spent that pays for itself in process efficiency.

Accounting, Finance & Planning

Does your company utilize an online application for handling employee expense reimbursement? Does the planning/budget process involve a system that roles up information based on reporting relationships, department hierarchies and/or job titles? Does Accounts Payable require and maintain manager approvals either in their systems or via manual reference? If so, then these too are opportunities to integrate H.R. information with business processes.

Start with identifying which *core data* elements are also housed in the Accounting/Finance systems.

These could include basics such as name, title, grade/band, supervisor, department and possibly salary. Obviously, the best scenario is to establish a regular feed from the H.R. *system of record* to the Accounting/Finance application. If this is not possible, then perhaps a monthly download-upload is feasible.

If no means exists to directly sync the system data in an electronic manner, then at the very least, consider a manual audit by printing out and comparing the information in each system prior to important events in the accounting process cycle. For example, a spot audit between H.R. records and the accounting hierarchy prior to the annual budget process could go a long way towards avoiding potential employee data discrepancies.

Property Mgmt / Real Estate

As briefly discussed in Section I, If your employer is large enough to have a Real Estate and/or Property Management office, then it's almost a certainty that they have established and are using some form of location code or Listing. When constructing a location *Schema* for headcount and other "people" reports, consider working with the Property Management and/or Real Estate departments to establish a common list of physical locations. Having H.R. and the Real Estate department already in alignment is helpful when selling in the simplified organizational reporting hierarchy (described in Chapter 2).

Procurement

Similar to the Accounts Payable functions, most Procurement and Purchasing functions require multi-level approvals. These controls are even more prominent since the onset of Sarbanes-Oxley.

Many Procurement departments maintain their own approval hierarchies separate from Human Resources processes and information. Not only is this an exercise redundancy, but the potential for incorrect information is obviously much higher.

Procurement approvals are frequently driven by job titles. For example, a particular spending threshold may require a Manager's approval, while a larger dollar amount demands clearance by a Director or even Vice President. Still other companies use a grade/band level rather than job title to administer consistent purchasing authority across the organization.

Once again, an automated real-time feed from H.R. systems to Procurement applications is always the best option, with the next best option being a periodic (weekly? monthly?) extract and upload between systems. Finally, when no automated technology is available, periodic printouts sent to Procurement for manual audit can still bring great value.

Summary

The key message of this chapter is that employee organizational data has use in business processes far beyond the H.R. Function. Leveraging employee and organizational data to help other departments optimize their processes then positions Human Resources as an important strategic business partner. Establishing this data continuity beyond Human Resources is also a proactive means for reducing discrepancies that ultimately reflect poorly on H.R. systems.

Section III:

The Best of The Rest!

*Rounding out the Fully Integrated
H.R. Department*

Section Introduction

There are a host of quasi-Human Resources functions that either make H.R. look really good when well executed or else exacerbate existing negative perceptions when they don't go well. These include things like tuition reimbursement, employee communication, training & development, employment verifications, etc.

Some H.R. leaders elect to disassociate their department from such tasks, citing them as "non-strategic" work. This can be a mistake for a couple of reasons. First, Human Resources is still associated with the tasks regardless of where the work gets pushed to. So H.R. credibility is still firmly attached to the outcome. Second, these processes hold valuable integration opportunities that can help basic H.R. processes function better.

This Section focuses on some of these processes that are often deemed "secondary" or even "quasi-H.R.", but are still essential to fully integrating the Human Resources Function.

Chapter #9: Training & Development

There are few expenditures that get greater scrutiny and incur more spending cuts during tough times than training & development activities. This is attributed at least in part to the:

> 1) Seemingly arbitrary nature that training funds get spent, and

> 2) Abstract "benefits" that training delivers to the organization.

Fortunately, using the proficiency catalog can assist with pulling training & development activities into the integration mix – thus helping (at least partially) with the effort to justify training costs.

Alignment of Training to Business Goals

Begin by identifying what skills are required – from the proficiency catalog – to reach the company's published strategy and/or fiscal year operational goals.

Next, map these Skills & Attributes to the training courses that are proposed for funding. While doing this may not necessarily translate into

measurement of hard dollar benefits, at least an argument can be made that the training is aligned to developing critical (skill/knowledge) enablers that support achievement of the company's strategic imperatives.

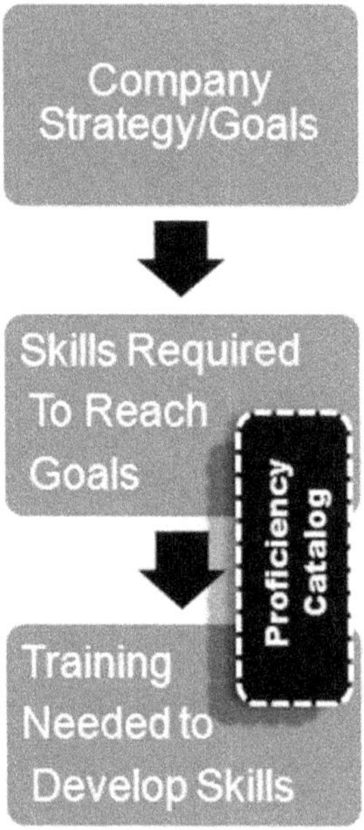

This may sound obvious to some readers, but it's amazing how many organizations expend valuable training resources without any formal linkage to how it helps the company achieve business goals. Even for those who have established competency models, Learning Management Systems and centralized training controls, there almost certainly is employee development going on in some corners of the organization that aren't formally aligned to business objectives.

ILLUSTRATION 9.1

Company Strategy/Goals

Skills Required To Reach Goals

Proficiency Catalog

Training Needed to Develop Skills

Eliminating Training Waste & Inefficiency

Another issue with training & development activities is the decentralized means by which processes are managed, and the degree to which they are (or shall we say "are not") leveraged across other H.R. processes. Do you hear about training going on in one part of the organization that seems similar to an initiative in another department? Do you have multiple Learning Management or delivery systems? Are you collecting all the data across the multiple training initiatives and/or systems and making use of it in your talent management initiatives? If not, then you have waste and inefficiency in your training & development efforts!

So what to do? Well if you do not already have centralized training function or Learning Management System (LMS), begin by researching and the establishing a catalog or inventory of all ongoing training initiatives throughout the organization. Next, map the documented training & development programs to the applicable Skills, Attributes and/or Functional Knowledge listings contained in the proficiency catalog. While nearly all training courses have some documented learning objectives clearly identified at the onset of the course, chances are this information does not align cleanly across multiple learning platforms.

Analyze this information to identify potentially duplicate training programs. A general guide is that if the course content and objectives are 80% or more the same, then a solid argument can be made for consolidation. Of course combining two training initiatives into one almost always equates to cost savings for the multiple departments who where individually funding duplicate training programs. While the individuals at the program delivery level may fall prey to the "no thanks...not invented here" mentality, chances are the department heads will applaud H.R.'s forward thinking that saved their precious budget dollars.

Harnessing Valuable Training Data

When H.R. training activities operate in separate silos, valuable data almost always remains in the LMS or manual training tracking mechanism (i.e. spreadsheets) which becomes limited to the department that administers the development activities. Tapping into training data can be a valuable decision making tool for

Compensation departments that serve as the gatekeeper for employee promotions. Likewise, the Recruiting group can utilize development information to take a forward looking approach at prospective internal candidates. Additionally, some organizations may include training & development data as part of talent inventory and succession processes.

For organizations that have multiple Learning Management Systems, or for that matter none at all, look in to establishing a process where each department administering training sends H.R. an update of their training records on a quarterly basis. Provide a data template that is comprised of the *core data* (established in Chapter 2), along with the actual training results. If the training has been inventoried and mapped to the categories in the proficiency catalog, (as described earlier in this chapter), then the administrative work on both ends of this task is minimal.

If the LMS or manual tracking tools don't contain the trainees' *core data*, then this is your chance to further the continuity of employee data across the entire organization! In such cases, the training administrator is often strapped with the task of manually maintaining the basic employee information in the tracking tool being used. Once again this is an opportunity for H.R. to position itself as a business partner by providing that information from the *System of Record* on a regular interval. Of course doing so means the department conducting the training must align their platform so the data synchronizes with the information received from H.R. systems.

 **When Recruiting Departments have access to Training & Development data, they can take a forward looking approach towards sourcing internal candidates.**

ILLUSTRATION 9.2

Integrating Learning Systems with H.R. Data

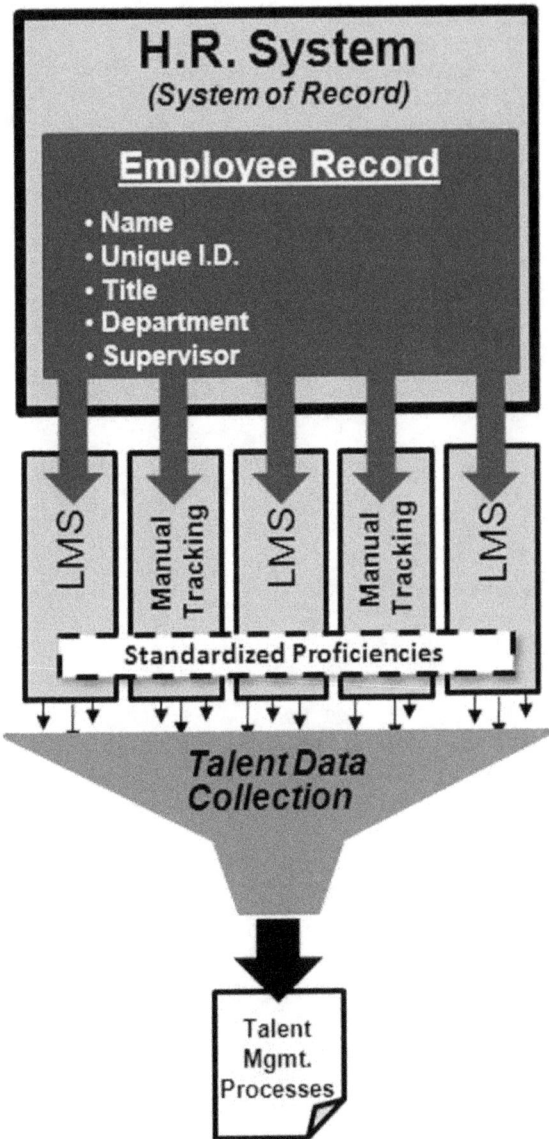

Chapter #10: Tuition Reimbursement, Employee Communications, etc.

Tuition Reimbursement

When the tuition reimbursement process is integrated, there are duel benefits. First, and most obvious, employees perceive H.R. as providing a very nice perk (regardless which department is actually paying the tab). Second, the process information can be used to update data needed for talent management activities.

Even if the Accounting department manages this function, have the program administrator produce a brief report on a regular basis (quarterly is probably sufficient) that indicates the employees who recently completed their degree. Then update this information in your H.R. or talent management system. (For some, the talent management "system" may be a spreadsheet or simple database. Either way, the principle still applies.) Performing these updates is an exercise in being proactive, and once established likely requires less than

30 minutes each calendar quarter. Remember, if you've applied the data management principles outlined in Section 1, then administrative tasks like this one that once took many hour are reduced dramatically! Little things that once were not worth the lengthy time investment suddenly become relatively small tasks.

Employee & Organizational Communication

Regardless of whether your Communications function resides in Human Resources or another part of the organization, it most certainly relies on employee data to effectively distribute messages to stakeholders. The degree to which this information is first accurate, and second accessible, directly affects how the Human Resources function is perceived in the company. In most cases, the Communications department (or whichever department is responsible for formal announcements) is the primary requestor of contact information for selected portions (and sometimes all) of the workforce. However, other departments such as Legal, Marketing, Real Estate/Property Management, Accounting/Finance or even Procurement may periodically seek organizational and employee contact information. These requests lend further credence to the principles (outlined in Chapter 2) regarding the pragmatic structuring of organizational hierarchies and the governance around whom and how workforce data can be used.

To further embrace the spirit with which this book has been created, it is worth noting that this provides yet another opportunity for process integration with respect to the company's employee directory. If the organization does make use of an intranet or other system for accessing employee contacts, then evaluate the need for identifying and contacting various sub-groups that comprise the workforce. Obviously, the ideal scenario is for stakeholders to be able to parse out the desired subgroups and pull the necessary contact information on their own.

Once again, such tasks may sound extremely basic and straight forward. And, for companies with well thought out data structures, integrated processes and top notch H.R. systems, this is certainly true. But there are challenges that may not be obvious at first. For example, is your employee directory structured in such a manner that allows stakeholders to produce contact information for:

- A professional subgroup such as the administrative/clerical employees across the entire organization

- All female or male employees

- Everyone within a specific section, department or division of the company

- All employees within a targeted geographic location.

These are just a few of the things to take into account when defining workforce data and configuring the integration of H.R. systems with the company's employee directory. Doing so not only empowers internal clients to obtain information on their own, thus reducing H.R. administrative work, it also becomes a direct reflection of how well Human Resources is viewed as a well organized operation and a provider of services that enable other departments with efforts to run the business. After all, isn't that what "strategic Human Resources is – or at least should be – all about?

Chapter #11: The Art of Generalist Transactions

If there ever was a black sheep in the H.R. family this would have to be it. Nobody wants to be responsible for any of the H.R. transactional work anymore. As Chief People Officers jump on the bandwagon to transform Human Resources into a "strategic function", two things are almost guaranteed to happen:

- There will be a major exercise to rename existing processes with new and more trendy monikers, and

4. There will be an effort made to push H.R. transactional work off to some other department or part of the organization.

What gets lost is that H.R. processes are only as good as the quality and efficiency of the routine employee transactions. Sending the work to the hiring manager, Accounting department or some other area is not likely to improve matters.

ILLUSTRATION 11.1

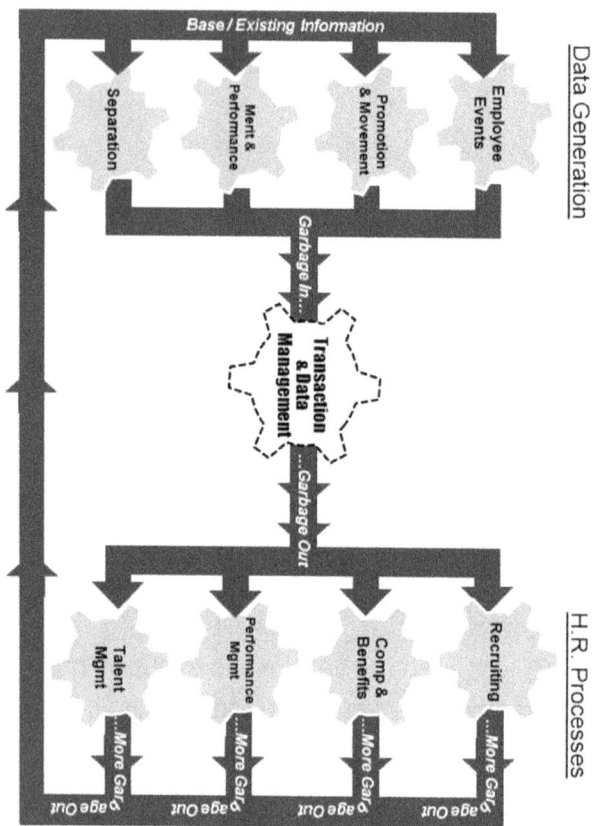

Rather than viewing this work as "non-value" added, H.R. leaders might do better to see transactional processes as powerful tools for transforming Human Resources into a strategic entity.

Remember that data is what drives all H.R. initiatives. Aligning transactional forms, processes and data controls on the front (transactional) end makes talent management activities easier to execute. And, the efficiencies don't stop there! If set up properly (see Section 1) then daily transactional work accumulates data in a manner that makes talent management analysis more streamlined. Some talent management administration is occurring automatically because it is embedded in the daily generalist transactional work.

And perhaps what the Human Resources profession has most lost sight of is this: When done accurately and efficiently, transactional work can in itself be a tremendous strategic enabler to the rest of the organization! Failure to view effective and efficient execution of basic employment lifecycle components as a strategic enabler is on par with refusing to see employees as organizational assets. Leaders need to spend less time on trying to shift transaction work out of H.R. and more energy on doing the same work more effectively.

> *Simplicity is the last step of art.*
>
> *Bruce Lee*

Chapter #12: A Final Word on H.R. Systems

H.R. Software Is Only Part Of The Solution

A well designed and fully integrated H.R. Information System can provide the framework to do much of what has been discussed in this book. In fact, many of the top applications available today are built upon the concept of integrating H.R. functions. Still there are plenty of companies that have top notch H.R. information systems yet still struggle with cross H.R. integration and overall process efficiency. That's because (at least in) the very best software is going to offer only marginal benefits if your processes and data aren't well defined. Plugging overly complex and/or fragmented processes into a software application gives you an electronic version of the same mess that existed prior to the technology investment. The same applies to the overall quality of your employee data.

Partner With Your I.T. Department

Once you've established a data dictionary and proficiency catalog, don't stop short of reviewing them with your I.T. department. Seek to establish a plan for configuring applicable fields in all H.R. applications to comply with the proficiency catalog. The goal is to deploy fixed selection criteria (i.e. drop down menus/lists) that conform to the proficiency catalog on as many systems and electronic documents as possible.

Such controls are particularly important for software where non-H.R. employees are entering and/or updating employee data. This might include individuals maintaining their own information in the employee directory, managers completing annual reviews, hiring managers posting resumes and various Employee-Manager Self Service applications.

Finally, don't forget to pull in any third party or outsourced providers as well. Examples may include benefits providers, payroll outsourcing and even regulatory reporting services.

One Good Reason

If you were only able to do ONE THING to improve the quality of your H.R. Reports and Metrics, the most important task just might be re-examining *reason codes* (or sometime referred to as employee events). This especially applies to larger organizations where there are many hundred hires, promotions, transfers, terminations a month.

I have personally witnessed organizations that have 50-60 unique codes. How many types of employee separations does your organization track? You are in good company if there is a sub-set of codes for voluntary departures, firings, layoffs, union vs. management, etc. In addition to bogging down transaction processing, the splintering of information also compromises the ability to look at what is going on regarding employee lifecycle trends throughout the organization.

The mistake made by many H.R. departments is the notion that more code selections create better gradient for examining the data. But, in reality, the fragmentation of the data actually makes it fuzzier. When there are too many options for classifying transaction information, then those completing the forms become indifferent about what they choose. Said more simply, if an organization has a 4-8 different *reason codes* that apply to employee transfers, then the probability of a transaction being incorrectly coded is much greater than if there were only 2-4 options. The same principle applies for all other transactions, including hires and especially separations, within the employee lifecycle.

Pairing down the list of codes is not an easy task. It's legitimate that legal/compliance functions, benefits administration, payroll processing and other workforce transactions all rely on highly specific classifications in order to manage effectively. The key is to get each representative group to maximize whatever opportunities exist for alignment to a common data *schema*. While all standardization efforts are usually painful, it can be tremendously helpful to have the I.T. department by your side as a co-sponsor of this initiative. After all, they have as much to gain from the added system continuity and simplicity as H.R. does in having standardized codes.

Aligning Non-H.R. Systems

In Chapter 8 we discussed increasing the value of H.R. information to the larger organization by feeding employee data to non-H.R. applications. Departments identified as having reliance on employee information included Procurement, Finance, Legal, Safety & Environmental Compliance and even I.T. However, it is also worthwhile to pursue aligning the configuration in these non-H.R. applications to the selection criteria standardized in certain portions of the proficiency catalog. For example, while there may be limited use for the Expertise lists outside of H.R., certainly there are applications that could be standardized on language, education, date fields and possibly functional groups.

Changing the coding/configuration is obviously an undertaking that must involve not only the department that "owns' the application, but also the I.T. department as well. Encouraging a multi-department system alignment initiative with a master plan co-lead by I.T. is the ideal scenario. If this isn't feasible, then at least push for alignment of employee data that exists outside H.R. systems.

 **Top Notch H.R. Software Systems are only partially effective if you don't also standardize, simplify and integrate your processes.**

Epilogue

Because each organization is in a unique place on their journey to maximizing H.R. effectiveness, and because both resources and challenges vary greatly by institution, it's natural that some readers will find more benefit from this book than others. But, at the very least I hope you close this last section with a renewed affirmation that GREAT THINGS CAN BE DONE THROUGH SIMPLE MEASURES!

Some readers will attempt to socialize the concepts in <u>The H.R. Predicament</u> with their department leaders, only to be told that the ideas are nice but nothing special. The unanswered question that will remain be, "then why aren't we doing it?"

The Human Resources as a profession must refocus on the basic elements that go into helping an organization maximize its human assets. We keep reaching for "seemingly" loftier roles in an attempt to be valued more by stakeholders. Yet, those initiatives will always be compromised (as well as harder and more resource intensive) if we aren't taking care of the basic H.R. functions needed throughout the daily operations of the organization.

Yes, we should aspire to higher and more strategic endeavors. However the approach should NOT be to abandon everyday services, but rather perform them in a manner that further enables these more advanced concepts.   This can only be sustainably achieved through internal H.R. process integration. And, **integration** can only realistically be obtained through **simplification**. These are the two underlying principles of this book.

My final advice regarding the information covered in The H.R. Predicament can best be summed up through the words of the great philosopher and martial artist Bruce Lee who said, "Absorb what is useful, discard what is not, add what is uniquely your own." (Lee)

INDEX

Bibliography / Works Cited

Aberdeen Group. (2006). *Succession Planning Benchmarking Report.* Boston.

Collison, J. (2007). *HR Technology Survey Report.* Alexandria, Va: SHRM.

Fegley, S. (2006). *Succession Planning Survey Report.* Alexandria, Va.: SHRM.

Fegley, S. (2006). *Talent Management Survey Report.* Alexandria, Va: SHRM.

Goldsmith, M. (2009). The 4 Tips For Efficient Succession Planning. *The Harvard Business Online* .

Lee, B. (1975). *The Tao of Jeetkunedo.* Santa Clarita, Ca.: Ohara Publications.

Thoreau, H. D. (1862). *Walking.* The Harvard Classics. New York,: P.F. Collier & Son Corporation.

Looking for help with
Standardizing, Simplifying
and Integrating your H.R.
Methods and Processes?

Visit www.iamproducts.net
to find out more how
Eric Schneider and
I Am Enterprises, LLC
can help!

www.ingramcontent.com/pod-product-compliance
Lightning Source LLC
Chambersburg PA
CBHW051524170526
45165CB00002B/592